India-Japan Relations in the Era of Globalisation

India-Japan Relations in the Era of Globalisation

Mohammed Badrul Alam

GYAN

First Published, 2018

Published by

Gyan Publishing House
5, Ansari Road
Daryaganj, New Delhi-110002
Phone: 9811692060
E-mail: books@gyanbooks.com

Printed at: G. Print Process, Delhi.

Cataloging in Publication Data—DK
Courtesy: D.K. Agencies (P) Ltd. <docinfo@dkagencies.com>

Alam, Mohammed Badrul, author.
India-Japan relations in the era of globalisation / Mohammed Badrul Alam.
pages cm
Includes bibliographical references.
ISBN 9788121214339 (HB)

1. India—Foreign economic relations—Japan. 2. Japan—Foreign economic relations—India. 3. India—Military relations—Japan. 4. Japan—Military relations—India. I. Title.

LCC HF1590.15.J3A43 2018 | DDC 338.9154052 23

Contents

Foreword

I am delighted that Professor Mohammed Badrul Alam is bringing out a volume titled "India-Japan Relations in the Era of Globalisation". It carries Articles on bilateral relations covering a wide span of themes including historic, security, economic, trade, investment, strategic, cultural *et al* by a string of eminent and erudite scholars and thinkers.

Much has been written on this extremely vital subject. Professor Badrul Alam's book however breaks new ground as it comes at a time when relations between India and Japan are soaring. It can be said safely that bilateral ties today are the best they have ever been. They enjoy the potential to scale even newer heights.

Bilateral ties between India and Japan have always been friendly and cordial. However, the energy and vigour evident on both sides to diversify and deepen partnership in a wide array of fields is something not witnessed in the past.

Launch of "Act East Policy" by Prime Minister Modi in November, 2014 to *inter alia* encompass Japan has infused greater dynamism and vitality to bilateral relations. This has been ably led by the two pro-active and visionary leaders like Narendra Modi and Shinzo Abe at the helm of affairs of the two countries. The rapid, assertive rise of China in political, military and economic spheres has also provided a context to the two countries to rapidly expand their partnership. Inclusion of Japan in the Malabar Naval Exercises between India and USA; initiation of quadrilateral discussions between USA, Japan, India and Australia at the recently held East-Asia Summit in Manila (12th November, 2017), and Asia Africa Growth Corridor are some recent developments which can be said to have been motivated by the China factor. The increasingly isolationist "America First" policies being pursued by USA under President Donald Trump have made it incumbent upon India and Japan to assume greater responsibility upon themselves to offer a push-back to China's aggressive posture as reflected in its Belt and Road initiative, South China Sea etc.

I am confident that Professor Mohammed Badrul Alam's effort will fulfill a much felt need to not only enumerate the current contours of the rapidly expanding partnership between India and Japan but will also provide a vision of their impact on security, peace and prosperity in Asia and the World.

I wish Professor Mohammed Badrul Alam all success.

Ashok Sajjanhar

Preface

The primary purpose of this book is to analyse, examine, evaluate and critique, and describe the emerging contours of India's foreign policy vis-à-vis Japan. India needs a closer relationship with Japan as the latter considers India as a viable partner which can facilitate intractable issues both in the South Asian region as well as beyond. India has never believed in the 'Big Brother policy' and 'hegemony' and has emphasised on bilateralism, regionalism and institutionalism as the tools for effective strengthening of relationship between India and Japan. Focusing on the re-orientation of the Indian foreign policy in the context of its relations with Japan, the book highlights the close historical, economic, political, commercial, strategic and cultural relations with national interests as the central foci.

The book is likely to generate immense academic, scholarly and public debate on issues related to the shaping of foreign policy of India with particular emphasis on its dealings with Japan. By discussing the impact of important bilateral measures with regional and sub-regional ramifications, the book provides a new vista and a possible paradigm shift which may have long terms implications for the South Asian regional architecture and beyond.

Chapter One argues that India's Act East Policy is a product of genuine synergy amongst its state stakeholders presumably under compulsive motivations and alignments of forces operating both within and outside the region. Mohammed Badrul Alam explains how a genuine change in mindset is imperative for regionalism and area study approach to emerge in the South Asian scene.

Chapter Two explains and critically analyse the strategic issues that are faced by both India and Japan. Masanori Kondo summarises as to how these issues have assumed new proportions after their switch in the regional and sub-regional context and thus ensuring both regional and state security from all sources at large.

Chapter Three provides a balanced and objective analysis as to how economic partnership between India and Japan has withstood the vicissitudes of times and multiple complex variables. Kojima Makoto surmises that continual partnership model could be a real panacea for linking both India and Japan strategically in the near to long term.

Chapter Four examines and evaluates the commonalities and the central role played by India in forging a close relationship with Japan for the evolution of regional order in Asia. Netajee Abhinandan elaborates how greater access to India in multiple arenas on the part of Japan can help to create a conducive environment for New Delhi-Tokyo partnership.

Chapter Five addresses the trajectory shift in the relationship as the security environment of a state is largely governed by its geographical location, which is closely linked to its domestic, regional and international setting. Raviprasad Narayanan surmises that India, in the short-term, should continue to provide the basis for ushering in strategic symmetry with Japan.

Chapter Six focuses on the continuous and cautious efforts made by India and Japan on maritime security. Akhter Hussain Khan describes the significance of maritime issues as it could be the tipping point for possible future great power rivalry in the oceans surrounding India and Japan.

Chapter Seven situates the India-Japan relations with perspective of international terrorism as its foci. Rajendra Kumar Pandey dwells on how in spite of onerous challenges, India-Japan relations has thrived well and looks promising in the joint war on terrorism front.

Chapter Eight examines how the China factor impacts both India and Japan. Gitanjali Sinha Roy discusses how the changing dynamics between India and Japan could be leveraged for a more predictable and benign outcome keeping the China's geo-strategic goals in mind.

Chapter Nine examines the geopolitical environment in Indi-Pacific region. Subhransu Sekhar Misra situates India-Japan relations within the changing contours of emerging and fast changing developments in the region.

Chapter Ten examines and evaluates India-Japan economic engagement with a neoclassicism perspective. R.P. Pradhan's chapter also addresses and delineates the role played by ASEAN in the emerging geo-politics of two nations.

Chapter Eleven highlights how Indo-Japan relations have been bound by commonalities over a wide range of issues ranging from efficacy of ASEAN and the need for Asian 'Balance'. Muzaffar Hussain describes how this bilateral relationship has serious ramifications for evolving power structure in Asia as well as for creation of regional architecture.

Chapter Twelve looks at the India's policy shift toward Japan from cordiality to estrangement to one of neutrality. Reyaz Ahmad Ganaie explains the need for safeguarding the core national interests while trying to avoid confrontation with China.

Chapter Thirteen discusses the salience of soft power in the context of Indo-Japan relations. Amit Kumar Gupta surmises that the quantum of soft power has enhanced the level of friendship thus leading to strong cultural and civilisational ties.

Mohammed Badrul Alam
Delhi

Acknowledgement

Mohammed Badrul Alam drew inspiration from teaching a wide range of students in India, USA and Japan over the past three decades. As for inculcation to foreign policy and American Studies discourse, it commenced long time ago in early 1980s in Jawaharlal Nehru University, New Delhi where he earned his M.Phil degree in American Studies at the School of International Studies. His professors, Dr B.K. Shrivastava, Dr M.S. Venkatramani and Dr R.P. Kaushik, taught him aspects and various nuances of foreign policy and American Studies and its implications. His long stint working at the Parliament Library, Teen Murti Nehru Memorial Library, American Center Library and ICWA Sapru House Library in New Delhi opened up his eyes to the scope and breadth of literature on almost all important facets of foreign policy, International Studies including strategic discourse.

In the United States, where Dr Badrul Alam attended Cornell University in Ithaca, New York, and earned his MA and PhD degrees in International Studies, many high profile professors such as Professor Mary Katzenstein, Prof. Milton Esman, Prof. Richard Polenberg, Professor Peter Katzenstein, Prof. Lawrence Scheinman, Professor Geroge McKahin, Prof. Benjamin Ginsberg, Prof. Richard Rosecrance, Prof Water LaFeber, instilled in him the various intricacies and complexities of issues related to India's foreign policy with its immediate neighbours.

In Japan, where he taught at Miyazaki International University in Southern Japan from 1998 to 2006, a number of colleagues such as Dr Kate Greenfield, Dr Getachew Felleke, Amanda Bradley, Dr Jeong Pyong-Hong, Dr Mika Mervio and Dr Yasu Izumikawa, helped Dr Alam in shaping his ideas and in bringing in the right focus on complex dynamics of India's foreign policy.

At Jamia Millia Islamia University, Delhi, where Dr Alam is presently a Professor of Political Science (and its Head, 2013-2016), all of his colleagues were of assistance in one way or the other. A number of his colleagues in the Department of Political Science including Prof. Rumki Basu, Prof. Nisar Ul Haq, Dr S.R.T.P.S. Raju, Jamia Millia Islamia's Pro-Vice Chancellor, Prof. Shahid Ashraf, Prof. Mujtaba Khan, OSD, Center for Distance and Open Learning at Jamia Millia Islamia and Prof. Sushant G. Ghosh, Director of Research at Jamia Millia Islamia, were great source of inspiration and motivation. A number of doctoral research scholars including Akhter Hussein Khan, Urvashi Shukeen, Zuhair Darzaid, Reyaz Ahmad Ganaie, Muzaffar Ahemad Ganaie, Akhilesh Tiwari, Digvijay Singh Sekhawat, Sarish Sebastian, Kuldeep Singh, Amit Gupta, were of immense help in collecting the source materials.

The greatest gratitude is owed to Dr Alam's father, Late Dr Sk. Islam and mother, Late Mrs. Hedatun Nisa Bibi, and brothers: Dr Mohammed Shamsul Alam and Mohammed Aminul Alam, and sisters: Dr (Mrs.) Swaleha Khatun, Mrs. Rahima Khatun, Mrs. Sofia Khatun, his wife: Mrs. Gahartaj Rokeya and the children: Saira Alam, Zubair Alam, Sadaf Alam and Munawar Alam. Although quite demanding and at times frustrating, everyone allowed him the time and necessary emotional support he needed to complete his work. Much of Dr Alam's success is due to their love and affection at all times.

Sincere thanks and deep appreciation are owed to Ambassador (Retd.) Shri Ashok Sajjanhar for consenting to write the Foreword of the book.

A special word of thanks to Shri Amit Garg, Director, Gyan Publishing House, New Delhi, India, for showing genuine interest in the manuscript and for its subsequent publication.

Professor Mohammed Badrul Alam

List of Contributors

- **Dr Mohammed Badrul Alam,** Professor, Dept. of Political Science, Jamia Millia Islamia University, New Delhi.
- **Dr Kojima Makoto,** Professor Emeritus, Takushoku University, Tokyo, Japan.
- **Dr Masanori Kondo,** Professor, Department of Economics and Business, International Christian University, Tokyo, Japan.
- **Dr Netajee Abhinandan,** Assistant Professor, Ravenshaw University, Cuttack, Odisha.
- **Dr Raviprasad Narayanan,** Associate Professor SIS, Jawaharlal Nehru University, Delhi.
- **Akhter Hussein Khan,** Ph.D Research Scholar, Dept. of Political Science, Jamia Millia Islamia, Delhi.
- **Dr Rajendra Kumar Pandey,** Assistant Professor Centre for Federal Studies, Jamia Hamdard, Delhi.
- **Gitanjali Sinha Roy,** Ph.D Research Scholar, Department of East Asian Studies, University of Delhi, Delhi.
- **Dr Subhransu Sekhar Misra,** Dept. of Political Science, National Defence Academy, Khadakwasla, Pune, India.
- **Dr R.P. Pradhan,** Associate Professor, Department of Humanities and Social Sciences, BITS (Goa Campus).
- **Dr Muzaffar Hossein,** Assistant Professor, Dept. of Political Science, MANUU, Arts & Science College for Women, Srinagar, J & K.
- **Dr Reyaz Ahmad Ganaie,** Assistant Professor, Dept. of Political Science, MANUU, Arts & Science College for Women, Srinagar, J & K.
- **Dr Amit Kumar Gupta,** Assistant Professor, Dept. of Political Science, Central University of Sikkim, Gangtok, Sikkim.

Chapter - 1

India's Act East Policy: An Overview of India-Japan Relations

---

—Mohammed Badrul Alam

This chapter shows that as part of India's overall 'Act East' policy, India and Japan are acutely aware of the need for strategic and security cooperation between the two countries for ensuring order, stability and equilibrium among the region's great powers. Both the countries recognise that India-Japan cooperation and the process of engagement cannot be sustained on sheer expediency, episodic and transactional basis but has to be firmly rooted in shared values in both security and strategic terms. In view of the economic opportunities and geo-strategic compulsions between India and Japan, one hopes that the same momentum would be carried forward in 2018 and beyond toward a new paradigm of mutual benefit.

Framing the relationship within Realist theoretical discourse of International Relations:

- "No nation can have a sure guide as to what it must do and what it need not do in foreign policy without accepting the national interest as that guide. ...Universal moral action cannot be applied to the action of states" (Hans J. Morgenthau, 1951).
- "The State's interests provides the spring of action" (Kenneth Waltz, 1979).
- "States seek power and they calculate their interests in terms of power" (Robert Keohane, 1986).

- "The international system is anarchic. The most basic motives driving states is survival" (John Mearsheimer, 1994).
- "States are motivated primarily by national interests" (Robert Gilpin, 1996).
- "Japan and India enjoy deep mutual understanding and are fully committed to enhance the strategic and global partnership for peace and prosperity" (Prime Ministers, Yoshihiko Noda and Dr Manmohan Singh, 2011).
- "With unwavering commitment to realise a peaceful, open, equitable, stable and rule-based order in the Indo-Pacific region and beyond, India and Japan uphold the principles of sovereignty and territorial integrity; peaceful settlement of disputes; democracy, human rights and the rule of law; open global trade regime; and freedom of navigation and overflight." (Prime Minister Narendra Modi and Prime Minister Shinzo Abe, 2015)

Power in the most generic term refers to the ability of influencing and articulating the behaviour of other states in order to achieve favourable outcome a state desires through attraction, inducement or coercion. Various national governments have at different times utilised their economic and military muscle in realising and enhancing their primary goals by increasing their raw power potential. The currency of power and security objectives are clearly evident in the twenty-first century globalised world with multiple transnational connectivity and changing contours of power. One can argue that India´s power has been enhanced in Asia Pacific in general and in context to East Asia and Japan in particular. In this context, foreign policy of India, like that of any other country, is shaped and influenced by geopolitics, geography, history, cultural parameters, and most importantly vital national interests with focus on 'Act East' policy. The changing economic, military and strategic environment in and around South Asia, South East Asia and East Asia has had its repercussions with India trying to reach out for new avenues for exercising greater mobility and flexibility in the regional sector for the conduct of its foreign policy. In this context, on one important issue, namely, the issue of nuclear proliferation as well as related security issues had its impact on India-Japan relations with profound policy ramifications.

Issue of Nuclear Proliferation and Related Security Issues

In view of the painful experience of being the only country in the world so far where nuclear bombs have been used to devastating effect, Japan has been overtly sensitive to any issues related to nuclear proliferation.

When India and Pakistan went for nuclear tests in May 1998, it was a rude shock to Japan's sensibilities. Along with other western countries and in particular the G-8 nations, Japan imposed severe economic sanctions on both India and Pakistan and accused them of flagrant violations of the letter and spirit of nuclear disarmament.

Japan, toward the end of 1999, provided indication in subtle terms to go soft on the continuance of economic sanctions on India. In an interview with ***Daily Asahi Shimbun***, Vice-minister Ichita Yamamoto expressed his satisfaction with New Delhi's "positive and forward-looking stance regarding signing CTBT and Japan's inching towards ending economic sanctions against India."(1)

In the aftermath of the terrorist incidents of September 11, 2001, both India and Japan came closer in cooperating in various facets of security perimeter affecting Central Asia, South Asia, South East Asia and East Asia. India had actively supported anti-terrorist stand taken by Japan and had lauded Japan's decision to send S.D.F (Self-Defense Force) units to the Arabian Sea and the Indian Ocean regions. India had also provided landing, refueling and docking facilities to Japanese fighter jets and ships.

In the foreseeable future in terms of security cooperation, Japan and India, are likely to have confined themselves to:

- Energy Security
- Maritime Security
- Enhanced contacts between the Armed Forces of the India and Japan

In all these three security fields, as Subash Kapilla analyses,(2) the operative principle should be that spheres of initiatives and cooperation are restricted to the bilateral context of Japan-India relations. The aim of Japan-India strategic cooperation should not be viewed to target containing China but moderating and engaging proactively China's approaches to Asian and East Asian Security to the extent possible under 'congagement'. Some observations from Kapilla are worth repeating, namely:

- Without getting overtly drawn into a United States- China strategic confrontation, countries such as Japan and India will be well advised to operate in close cooperation and in sync with each other and which could hopefully provide necessary counter-ballast for ensuring peace and stability in the Asia-Pacific.
- With Japan and India opting for strategic cooperation, the third big Asian power i.e. China would consequently afford much needed strategic space to these two powers and thereby paving the way for a balanced Asian Security.

Recognising that India and Japan have large Exclusive Economic Zones and maritime interests (including safe passage or Japanese oil tankers plying from the Persian Gulf to Strait of Malacca through Arabian Sea, Indian Ocean and Bay of Bengal under protection from Indian Navy and its Coast Guards) there is a need for enhance cooperation in capacity building, technical assistance and information and data sharing between their respective agencies and undertake anti-piracy measures in the high seas. It includes shared commitment by both India and Japan to maritime security, freedom of navigation and overflight, civil aviation safety, unimpeded lawful commerce, and peaceful settlement of disputes in accordance with international law.

Similarly, regular exchange visits between the two Coast Guards through meetings of heads of Coast Guards, mutual visits of Coast Guard ships and holding of combined exercises are very important for both India and Japan in strengthening their respective security perimeters. In this context, the signing of a Memorandum on Cooperation between the Coast Guards was welcomed. Coming into force of the Regional Cooperation Agreement on Combating Piracy and Armed Robbery against Ships in Asia (ReCAAP) and reaffirming to enhance cooperation in respect of anti-piracy countermeasures under its framework are welcome measures in this direction.

Japan and India condemn terrorism in all its forms and manifestations and stress that there can be no justification whatsoever for any act of terrorism. They share the view that international community must further intensify all out efforts and cooperation to fight this menacing threat to global peace and security. In this context, the two countries have pledged to work in unison through the India-Japan Joint Working Group on Counter Terrorism. Both Japan and India have also called upon all Member States of the UN to work towards the expeditious adoption of a Comprehensive Convention on International Terrorism.(3)

The big leap in the Relationship in the Twenty-first Century and the Future

In contemporary times, from the time of Yoshiro Mori as Prime Minister in August 2000, subsequent Japanese prime ministers in the recent past have shown real enthusiasm and made tangible efforts for the improvement of relationship with India.

After the mutual warmth in the 1950s during the Nehru era, India and Japan drifted apart during the Cold War.(4) Shinzo Abe during his landmark August 2007 visit to India, however, traced his personal affinity towards India to the sentimental visit of his grandfather and prime minister of Japan, Nobusuke Kishi, who arrived in India during 1957 to a friendly reception from Jawaharlal Nehru. Abe reciprocated this great gesture by inviting Prime Minister Dr Manmohan Singh to Tokyo in December 2006 and in arranging a speech made by Dr Singh to members of Japanese Diet and a rare audience with the Japanese emperor. Subsequently, Dr Singh made official visits to Japan in 2008 and 2010 as well geared toward advancement of strategic and economic partnership between India and Japan. This was followed with their meeting in Tokyo on 1 September 2014 and that was followed by their meeting in Delhi in 12 December 2015 between Prime Minister Narendra Modi and Prime Minister Shinzo Abe wherein both leaders pledged to realise the full potential of India-Japan Strategic and Global Partnership for continuing progress and prosperity for their respective people and for advancing peace, stability and prosperity in Asia and the world. Elevating the relationship to a Special Strategic and Global Partnership, they called their meeting the dawn of a new era in India - Japan relations. Both sides also agreed to build complementary skills and resources to build a strong partnership to promote economic and social development, capacity-building and infrastructure development in other interested countries and regions.

Second, Indian political elite has increasingly looked to Japan as it steered Japan towards a new proactive role and has looked at India as a hard power of 'coercion', soft power of 'attraction' and cultural superpower of 'inducement' in Asia and the world. New generation of leaders in Tokyo believed that Japan should shed its defensive posture about its imperial past and become a "normal" power. From Abe to Noda to Abe II, each of the Prime Ministers was also pressing ahead with Junichiro Koizumi's agenda of unshackling Japan from its post Second World War political limitations and constitutional inhibitions on taking new, visible security responsibilities in Asia and beyond.

Third, the rise of China in recent years has compelled Japan to re-evaluate its own long-term options in Asia that many expect would inevitably become Sino-centric for maximising Chinese national interests. As Japan, much like the United States, hedges its bets against the rise of China including its assertiveness on matters related to South China Sea and Senkaku/Diaoyu island, political and security cooperation with India has become imperative of Japan's new grand strategic calculus. However, Japan's new emphasis on a "global and strategic partnership" with India by no means implies that the two want to ally against China. In an age of rapid economic integration in Asia, China is already the largest trading partner of Japan and is set to acquire a similar status with India. The focus of both New Delhi and Tokyo is on widening the window of flexibility and opportunity in their conduct of foreign and security policies in Asia rather than seek an impossible containment of China that would provide no benefits to any party either in the short-term or long-term.

Fourth, while China will remain the key partner for Japan, Tokyo under Shinzo Abe is inclined to invest and enter into another important economic relationship for a possible multi-polar Asia. As a consequence, India has overtaken China as the largest recipient of Japan's overseas development assistance. As Japan has fallen behind China and Korea in taking advantage of India's economic reforms, Abe has highlighted the need for engaging India and its emerging economy with all its might in the fast changing power game in Asia-Pacific.

Finally, for the first time in the last sixty years, Prime Minister Shinzo Abe has injected the notion of shared and complementary political values into the bilateral discourse. Despite being two major working democracies in the world, the common vision to democracy has never figured in India-Japan relationship. With a firm commitment to openness and constructive engagement, the Indo-US nuclear deal, for example, promises to change New Delhi's standing in the global nuclear order and with Japan providing a helping hand to harness India tap nuclear energy in its civilian sector. In the areas of Civil Nuclear Energy, Non-proliferation and Export Control, during Prime Minister Modi's visit to Japan in September 2014 and Abe's return visit to Delhi in 2015, both sides have affirmed the importance of civil nuclear cooperation between the two countries and welcomed the significant progress in negotiations on the Agreement for Cooperation in the Peaceful Uses of Nuclear Energy. They directed their officials to further accelerate the negotiations with a view to concluding the Agreement at an early date, and strengthen the two countries' partnership in non-proliferation and nuclear safety. While Prime Minister Abe commended India's efforts in the field of non-proliferation including the affirmation that goods and technologies transferred from Japan would not be used for delivery systems for WMD, Prime Minister Modi appreciated the decision of the Government of Japan to remove six of India's space and defence-related entities from Japan's Foreign End User List. They looked forward to enhanced trade and collaboration in high technology. Both sides also affirmed their commitment to work together for India to become a full member in the four international export control regimes: Nuclear Suppliers Group, Missile Technology Control

Regime, Wassenaar Arrangement and Australia Group, with the aim of strengthening the international non-proliferation efforts.

As Asia, the largest continent, undergoes major transformation in terms of power configurations, India and Japan are acutely aware of the need for political and security cooperation between the two countries for ensuring order, stability and equilibrium among the region's great powers. Both the countries recognise that India-Japan cooperation and process of engagement cannot be sustained on sheer expediency but has to be firmly rooted in shared values in both economic and strategic terms. That precisely is why Narendra Modi and Shinzo Abe found it so important to emphasise nourishment of democracy and liberal democratic values as the future bilateral political glue between the two Asian powers. As a follow up to the highly successful Modi's visit to Japan in September 2014, Minister for Foreign Affairs, Fumio Kishida held the Eighth Japan-India Foreign Ministers' Strategic Dialogue with Mrs. Sushma Swaraj, External Affairs Minister of India on January 17, 2015, wherein both the sides agreed to enhance connectivity within SAARC (the South Asian Association for Regional Cooperation) and to work together to strengthen connectivity between SAARC and ASEAN (the Association of Southeast Asian Nations). Both India and Japan also affirmed the promotion of political dialogue including Japan-India-U.S. trilateral cooperation, and security cooperation such as joint maritime exercises and continuation of 2+2 dialogue, a formal bilateral framework between their foreign and defense ministers. They also discussed several important bilateral as well as regional and global issues. Both sides reaffirmed that Japan and India as partners share common values and strategic interests and have made a strong commitment to develop the Strategic and Global Partnership further for the deepening of their bilateral relations as well as peace and prosperity of the region and the world.(5) As the joint statement between Prime Minister Modi and Abe that was issued at the end of Japanese Prime Minister Shinzo Abe's visit to India on 14 September 2017 stated, there is "growing convergence in the political, economic and strategic interests, based on the firm foundation of common values and traditions, as well as on an emerging consensus on contemporary issues of peace, security and development."(6) In view of economic opportunities and geo-strategic compulsions between India and Japan, one hopes that under Japan's current Prime Minister Shinzo Abe's stewardship and that of India's Prime Minister Narendra Modi, the same momentum would be carried forward in 2018 and beyond toward a new paradigm of mutual benefit on a win-win proposition.

Notes

An earlier version of the chapter appeared in *Emerging India in the New World Order*, editors, Mohammed Badrul Alam and Nisar ul Haq, Bloomsbury Publishing India Pvt. Ltd; Delhi, 2015.

1. ***India Today***, New Delhi, November 15, 1999, "Japan urges Pakistan to restore democracy, sign CTBT", http://www.india-today.com/intoday/newsarchives/99/11/15/n45.shtml, see, Miyashita, Akitoshi and Yoichiro Sato(eds.), *Japanese Foreign Policy in Asia and the Pacific*, New York: Palgrave Publications, 2001, also, see, Sanjana Joshi, *Changing Japan: Opportunities and Challenges for India*, Delhi: Shipra Publications, 2008; Takenori Horimoto and Lalima Varma (eds.), *India-Japan Relations in Emerging Asia*, New Delhi: Manohar, 2013; Srabani Roy Choudhury (ed.), *Japan-SAARC Partnership: A Way Ahead*, Delhi: Pentagon Press, 2014; G. Balachandirane (ed.), *Japan in a Resurgent Asia*, Delhi: Manak Publications, 2010; M.D. Dharamdasani, *Indo-Japan Relations: Challenges and Opportunities*, Delhi: Kanishka Publishers, 2004.
2. Dr Subash Kapilla, "Japan-India Strategic Dialogue: A Misnomer", South Asia Analysis Group, Paper No. 2187, 29.03.2007, see, also, *The Japan Times*, February 15, 2012, http://www.japantimes.co.jp/text/nb20120215d1.html
3. From, Rediff.com, December 15, 2006, "India, Japan to establish Strategic Partnership", http://www.rediff.com/news/2006/dec/15ind.htm, also, see, Brahma Chellaney, "India-Japan Relationship: Shard Values to Shared Interests", *The Economic Times*, Delhi, December 29, 2011.
4. C. Raja Mohan, "Visit of the Rising Ties", *The Indian Express*, New Delhi, December 14, 2006, http://www.indianexpress.com/story/18476.html, see, Panda, Rajaram and Yoo Fukazawa (eds.), *India and Japan: Blossoming of a New Understanding*, New Delhi: Lancer Books, 2004, also, see, Dharmdasani, M.D, *Indo-Japan Relations: Challenges and Opportunities*, New Delhi: Kanishka Publishers, 2004, see, Jithin George, "India-Japan Relations at 60: Setting the Stage for Kizuna", Institute of Peace and Conflict Studies, Delhi, Article No. 3561, 20 January 2012, http://www.ipcs.org/article/india/india-japan-relations-at-60-setting-the-stage-for-kizuna-3561.html

5. *Ibid,* C. Raja Mohan, No. 4, also, see, http://www.mofa.go.jp/region/asia-paci/india/pmv0912/joint.html , see, *The Times of India*, September 1, 2014, http://timesofindia.indiatimes.com/india/Tokyo-Declaration-for-India-Japan-Special-Strategic-and-Global-Partnership/articleshow/41433328.cms, also, see, Ministry of Foreign Affairs, Tokyo, web site, January 18, 2015, www.mofa.go.jp/s_sa/sw/in/page3e_000295.html, September 9, 2016, http://www.mofa.go.jp/s_sa/sw/in/page3e_000430.html, also, See, *The Diplomat*, September 5, 2016, http://thediplomat.com/tag/india-japan-relations/
6. See, Joint Statement, http://www.mofa.go.jp/files/000289999.pdf; September 14, 2017.

References

C. Raja Mohan, "Visit of the Rising Ties", The *Indian Express*, New Delhi, December 14, 2006.

Dharmdasani, M.D, *Indo-Japan Relations: Challenges and Opportunities*, New Delhi: Kanishka Publishers, 2004.

Drifte, Reinhard, *Japan's Foreign Policy in the 1990s: From Economic Super Power to What Power?,* London: Macmillan Press, 1996.

Jain, Purnendra C.(ed.), *Distant Neighbours: Japan and South Asia*, New Delhi: Sterling Publishers, 1996.

Keshavan, K.V(ed.), *Building a Global Partnership: Fifty Years of Indo-Japanese Relations*, New Delhi: Lancer Books, 2002.

Lim Hua Sing, *Japan's Role in Asia: Mutual Development and Ruthless Compeition*, Singapore: Eastern University Press, 2003.

Masako Fukuda, "India Blasts Fire up Resistance to Nuclear Weapons in Japan", *Nikkei Weekly*, 18 May 1998, p.1.

Mattoo, Amitabh, "India's Strategic and Foreign Policy Perceptions", in Keshavan, K.V(ed.), *Building a Global Partnership: Fifty Years of Indo-Japanese Relations*, New Delhi: Lancer Books, 2002.

Miyashita, Akitoshi and Yoichiro Sato (eds.), *Japanese Foreign Policy in Asia and the Pacific*, New York: Palgrave Publications, 2001.

Murthy, P.A. Narasimha, *India and Japan: Dimensions of their Relations*, New Delhi: Lancer Books, 1993.

Panda, Rajaram, *Japan and the Third World: Political and Economic Interactions 1980s-1990s*, New Delhi: Lancer Books, 1994.

Panda, Rajaram and Kazuo Ando (eds.), *India and Japan Multi-dimensional Perspectives*, New Delhi: Lancer Books, 1997.

Panda, Rajaram and Yoo Fukazawa (eds.), *India and Japan: Blossoming of a New Understanding*, New Delhi: Lancer Books, 2004.

Rajesh Kapoor, "Dawn of a New Era in India-Japan Relations", Institute of Peace and Conflict Studies, New Delhi, Article No. 2177, 4 January 2007.

Rukmani Gupta, "PMs Japan Visit", Institute of Peace and Conflict Studies, New Delhi, Article No.2185, 9 January 2007.

Dr Subash Kapilla, "Japan-India Strategic Dialogue: A Misnomer", South Asia Analysis Group, Paper No. 2187, 29.03.2007.

Wolf Mendel, *Japan's Asia Policy: Regional Security and Global Interests*, New York: Routledge, 1995.

Chapter - 2

Japan–India Economic Partnership: Strategic Linkages

—*Makoto Kojima*

Japan and India have a long history of economic interaction as natural partners. They became economically estranged from each other since the mid-1960s, but a new tide has risen in Japan–India relations since the mid-2000s. India has become the largest recipient of Japanese ODA since 2003. Bilateral trade began to show a rising trend, with Comprehensive Economic Partnership Agreement (CEPA) coming into effect in 2011. Japanese foreign direct investment (FDI) into India has shown a conspicuous expansion since 2008, which is highly anticipated as force bolstering the Indian manufacturing sector.

In 2006, Japan and India entered into their Strategic and Global Partnership against the backdrop of geopolitical change triggered by China's emergence, which provided a framework for long-term cooperation in both economic and security related fields. Their annual summit meeting has been instrumental in implementing bilateral collaboration in Indian infrastructure. The Delhi–Mumbai Industrial Corridor (DMIC) project, with the Western Dedicated Freight Corridor (DFC) as its backbone, serves as an important symbol of advanced bilateral collaboration related to Indian infrastructure development.

The formation of the Modi government has provided momentum bolstering Japan–India economic relations. The bilateral relationship was elevated in 2014 to a Special Strategic and Global Partnership. Various initiatives have been undertaken under the Modi government to revive strong economic growth. Currently, India enjoys economic growth that is among the highest in the world, and views Japan as a key partner for his strategy to promote economic modernisation and infrastructure development. Examining the latest features of Japan–India economic relations, this chapter will point out the new direction of bilateral economic partnership in a new Asian era.

I. Japan-India Trade on a Modest Growth

Before World War II, India had been Japan's major trade partner, accounting for 10–15 per cent of Japan's foreign trade up until 1937. Major imported products from India were cotton and pig iron. Japan and India were mutual competitors in textile and steel industries. Notably, Japan and India were not only competitors, but also good partners. Tata, an Indian conglomerate, and Nippon Yusen Kaisha (NYL Line) collaborated in launching regular services between Bombay and Kobe in 1892 in rivalry with P&Q, enabling Japan to import raw cotton at a reasonable cost.

After World War II, India remained an important trade partner of Japan, accounting for 2–4 per cent of trade until around 1965. In the post-war era, iron ore replaced pig iron as the major imported product from India. It played a crucially important role in the remarkable post-war development of the Japanese steel industry until Japan started to import iron ore on a large-scale from Australia and Brazil. Since the mid-1960s, under its closed inward-looking regime, India has struggled with industrial stagnation and has been left behind by the global tide. Japan, in contrast, joined the Organisation for Economic Co-operation and Development (OECD) in 1964. It has ridden the track of high-speed economic growth, becoming an economic superpower. Japan's economic relations with Asian countries increasingly emphasized East Asian countries. Since then, Japan and India have become economically estranged from each other.

Along with the introduction of economic reforms in 1991, India adopted an outward-looking policy to stimulate its own economy using the tide of globalisation. Japan–India economic relations showed signs of expansion in the 1990s, but were set back in 1998 because of Japan's sanctions against India related to its conduct of nuclear tests. It was only in 2003-04 that bilateral trade started to present an upward trend, increasing from US$5.36 billion to US$18.51 billion in 2011-12.

Improved bilateral trade, however, has stagnated since then and has been largely overshadowed by other bilateral trading relations such as those of India with ASEAN, China, and Korea. In fact, Japan–India bilateral trade was surpassed by India–China trade in 2002-03 and by India–Korea trade in 2005-06. Under the "Look East Policy", India–China and India–ASEAN trade had quadrupled relative to Japan (Figure 1). Japan's share in all Indian trade declined from 5.9 per cent in 1997-98 to 2.1 per cent in 2016-17, with Japan's rank in total Indian trade declining from third in the mid-1990s to thirteenth in 2016-17. India's share of Japan's total amount of trade remained at only one per cent in recent years.

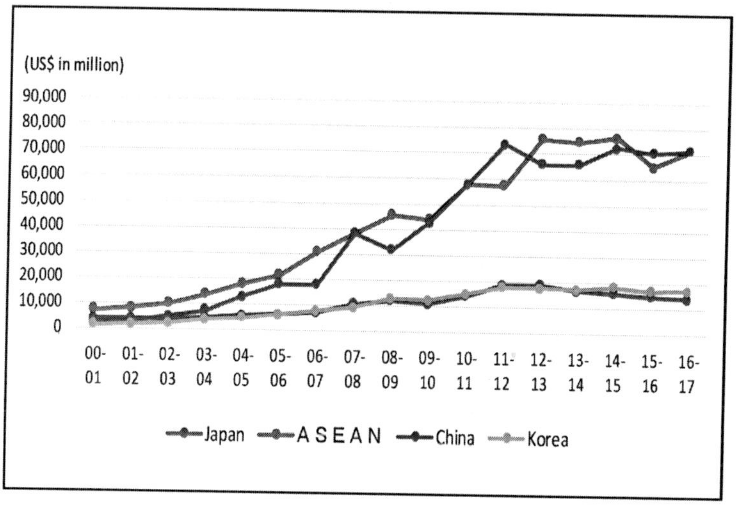

Source: Ministry of Commerce and Industry, Export Import Data Bank.

Figure 1: India's Trade with East Asia.

The Japan–India Comprehensive Economic Partnership Agreement (CEPA) came into effect in August 2011. Under the Japan–India CEPA, tariffs on 90 per cent of Indian and 97 per cent of Japanese goods have been scheduled for elimination over the course of ten years. Auto components, iron and steel products, electric and electronics parts, and general machinery are included in concessionary import items on the Indian side. Regarding concessionary import items on the Japanese side, the tariff rate for almost all goods in industrial and mining industries imported from India would be eliminated immediately. Japan–India bilateral trade jumped from US$13.72 billion in 2010-11 to US$18.51 billion in 2011-12 and US$18.52 billion in 2012-13. Since then, it has decreased to US$13.60 billion in 2015-16. Given that India's total trade has also been shrinking since 2011-12, it might be too early to appraise the effects of the CEPA on the status of Japan–India trade, but its impact has not been favourable so far. Here, we can point out the following three challenges facing current Japan–India bilateral trade.

First, Japanese exports to India have been overwhelmed by a sweeping expansion of Chinese exports to India. China has successfully penetrated the Indian market with low-priced goods even without enjoying any benefit under the CEPA. The example of Japanese exports of steel products to India is illustrative. Hot and cold rolled steel plates, alloy steel and galvanised steel sheet have been scheduled for exemption from five per cent tariffs within five years. Japanese exports of steel products increased from US$1.37 billion in 2010-11 to US$2.08 billion in 2012-13, but thereafter decreased to US$0.93 billion in 2016-17. By contrast, Chinese steel products exports to India averaged at almost US$3 billion during the period between 2010-11 and 2016-17.

Second, Japan and India have yet to form such mutual horizontal trade. Petroleum products, notably naphtha, accounted for almost 15 per cent of India's exports to Japan in 2016-17, followed by organic chemicals, marine products, and precious stones. Japan has expanded its horizontal trade relationship with East Asian countries, engendered by extending its production network across borders. Therefore, the expansion of Japanese foreign direct investment (FDI) into India holds the key to the expansion of trade between the two countries because it paves the way for India to be incorporated into the existing East Asian production network, thereby building horizontal trade between the two countries.

Third, India is a country that has a strong advantage in manufacturing pharmaceutical products, especially generic medicines, which constitute India's second most important export items to the

US, following precious stones. Under the Japan–India CEPA, national treatment is to be accorded between the two countries for application for registration and other approvals required for the release of generic medicines. Nevertheless, there are still many hurdles to overcome in Japan to expand the import of pharmaceutical products from India. India's exports of pharmaceutical products to Japan increased from US$13.8 million in 2010-11 to US$66.96 million in 2012-13, but stagnated at US$40.43 million in 2016-17. Considering that the Japanese government intends to increase the share of generic medicine from 56.2 per cent in 2015–2016 to more than 80 per cent by 2020-21 from the standpoint of checking ballooning medical expenditures, there should be much possibilities for the expansion of imports of generic medicines from India under the Japan–India CEPA framework.

II. New Horizons for Japanese FDI into India

(1) Surge of Japanese FDI into India

It is in the area of investment that Japan–India economic relations have experienced a more dynamic trend. Japanese companies used to be reluctant about investing into India, having a negative image of India's investment environments that constituted a sense of "psychological distance" from India. That reluctance notwithstanding, faced with stagnant markets in economically advanced countries and aggravated investment environments in China, where wages are rising and industrial policies becoming more restrictive and unpredictable for foreign companies, India has become more attractive in Japanese business circles. In addition, Korean companies' success in gaining a larger share of consumer electronics reflects that Japanese companies' areas of concern, e.g. adverse investment environments, are not necessarily important factors.

Japan ranked third after Mauritius and Singapore, accounting for eight per cent of the total accumulated volume of FDI inflows into India from April 2000 to March 2017. India accounts for only 1.3 per cent of Japan's total outward FDI stock at the end of 2016. Since 2009, Japanese FDI into India began to show conspicuous expansion, Japanese FDI into India increased from US$ 405 million in 2006-07 to US$2,972 million in 2011-12 (Fig. 2). Although

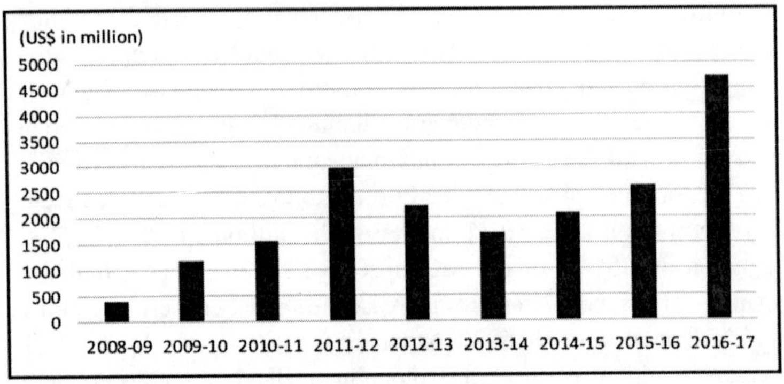

Source: Ministry of Commere and Industry, Fact Sheet of FDI.

Figure 2: Japanese FDI into India.

declining to US$1,718 million in 2013-14, it rose again to US$ 4,709 million in 2016-17.

An increasing trend in Japanese FDI into India is also reflected in the number of Japanese companies operating in India. From October 2008 to October 2016, the number of Japanese companies increased from 362 to 1305, with the number of their establishments increasing from 836 to 4590 (Fig. 3). It is noteworthy that some discrepancy exists in data related to Japanese FDI into India between the two countries. According to the net flow-based FDI data compiled by the Japanese Ministry of Finance, Japanese FDI into India increased from the US$500 million level in 2006 to the US$1,500 million level in 2007. Reflecting Daiichi Sankyo's acquisition of the Indian largest pharmaceutical company of Rambaxy, and NTT DOCOMO's purchase of the shares of Tata Teleservices, Japanese FDI into India culminated to US$5.55 billion in 2008 and US$3.66 billion in 2009, comparable to the level of Japanese FDI into ASEAN and China. Thereafter, Japanese FDI into India stagnated at the US$2 billion level, left far behind Japanese FDI into ASEAN and China. After marking minus US$1.71 billion, reflecting Daiichi Sankyo's withdrawal of its investment from India, Japanese FDI into India recovered to US$3.69 billion in 2016[1].

In the past, Japanese FDI into India had been geared toward the manufacturing sector, attracting 76 per cent of the total Japanese FDI

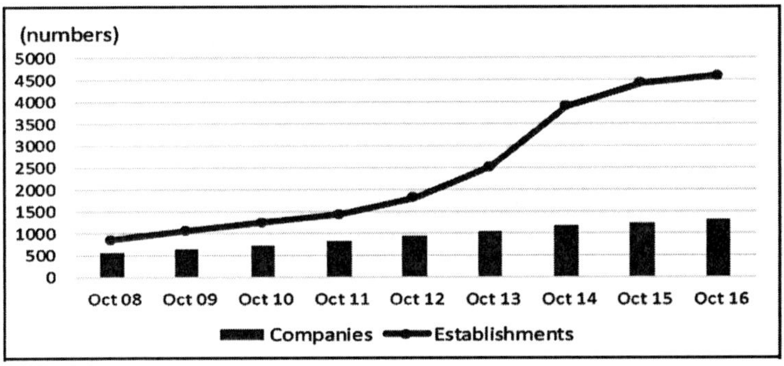

Source: Japanese Embassyin India

Figure 3: Number of Japanese Companies in India.

stocks into India as of 2016. Looking at the sub-sector level, transport machinery, mostly automobiles and automobile parts, accounted for 42 per cent of the total Japanese FDI into India. Major Japanese assemblers including Suzuki, Nissan, Toyota and Honda have marked India as a strongpoint for the production of small cars and sport utility vehicles (SUVs) in their global strategy. Japanese FDI has been instrumental in bolstering the Indian manufacturing sector by bringing a high-quality production base and upgrading the skill-levels of labourers. It is noteworthy that a growing number of Indian manufacturers have been awarded the prestigious Japanese Deming Prize for their contributions to the field of total quality management (TQM)[2].

Japanese automobile assemblers and auto part manufacturers' firm presence strongly induce other companies involved in steel, machines, power plants, and logistics to come to India. Regarding the electronics appliance sector, Panasonic, Daikin and Sony have exerted strenuous efforts to catch up with LG and Samsung, and have been backed with strong commitment from top management. Japanese companies have also forayed into sectors such as pharmaceuticals, foods, retails, stationery, cosmetics, and sanitary goods. For example, Ryohin Keikaku operator of Muji brand, has already opened its stores in Mumbai and Delhi in 2016 and 2017 under a joint venture with Reliance Brands, and First Retailing, operator of the Uniqro casualwear brand, will soon open its stores in India. Soft Bank is already one of the largest investors in India's ecommerce market.

Japanese financial institutions including insurance companies are also engaged in vigorous activities in the Indian financial market, with their investment amounting to 24 per cent of the total Japanese FDI stocks into India. Given that infrastructural development projects require a huge amount of capital and knowing that Indian companies actively raise funds in global capital markets, Japanese financial institutions have recognised the Indian market as an important target. They have furnished funds to Indian companies.

Convinced that India offers a huge domestic market and that it will emerge as a leading economic power, Japanese companies have become increasingly committed to India, not only for supplying for a huge domestic market, but also for setting up production bases for global markets and R&D centres.

(2) Prospects and challenges for additional Japanese FDI into India

According to surveys conducted by the Japan Bank for International Cooperation (JBIC) related to promising countries for business operations for Japanese manufacturing companies, India has ranked first on a long-term perspective since 2010. Moreover, the latest surveys conducted in 2014, 2015 and 2016 have shown that India is ranked first not only on the long-term for the next ten years, but also on a medium-term for the next three years, indicating that Japanese companies hold strong expectations for India as an investment destination. The main reasons for India being promising include the enormous future growth potential of the local market; the huge size of the current local market; the inexpensive supply of abundant labour; the established supply base of assemblers; and its promising location as a base of export to third countries. Nevertheless, many issues persist on the part of India for attracting FDI, including underdeveloped infrastructure; unclear execution of its legal system; intense competition with other companies; its complicated tax system; and issues of security and social instability.

India is ranked at 100 by the World Bank Doing Business 2018 ranking among 190 countries (benchmarked to June 2017), which indicates that the investment climate in India still presents harsh conditions, although it moved up in its ranking conspicuously from the previous year's position of 130. It is very often the case that Japanese small and middle enterprises (SMEs) hesitate at investing into India because of underdeveloped infrastructure in the fields of the power sector and logistics. To address issues of unclear execution of its legal system and complicated tax system, foreign investors are well advised to tie-up with reliable local partners. Furthermore, given that India's industrial base is widely established, and that both local and multilateral companies are vigorously pursuing their business activities, foreign investors find themselves surrounded by tough competitors in the Indian market, further exacerbating India's severe business climate.

Currently, as many as eleven "Japan Industrial Townships (JITs)" are being set up in eight states, with a view to addressing the various issues confronting Japanese investors in India, including such problems related to underdeveloped infrastructure, land acquisition, and complicated clearances, which might be extremely helpful for Japanese SMEs to invest into India. The industrial park in Nimurana, Rajasthan is already under operation.

Following Prime Minister Narendra Modi's visit to Japan in September 2014, a special cell known as "Japan Plus" was set up under the Government of India to facilitate and fast track investment proposals from Japan. The cell is placed under the Department of Industrial Policy and Promotion (DIPP), Ministry of Commerce and Industry. The team comprises six members: four from the Government of India and two from Japan's Ministry of Economy and Industry (METI). The decision to place members of a foreign government within a unit under the Government of India is unusual, and indicates that both Japanese and Indian Governments are engaged in close cooperation for facilitating Japanese investment into India.

Aside from issues related to the investment climate in India, the difference of corporate culture between the two countries poses another challenge for Japanese FDI into India. From Indian eyes, Japanese companies tend to be risk averse. Moreover, they are shy about committing themselves deeply to local Indian businesses from a long-term perspective. Differences in negotiation styles sometimes become obstacles to reaching agreements between the two sides. When starting a negotiation, the Indian side tends to prioritize the establishment of a basic agreement with subsequent formal negotiations for discussing detailed matters, whereas the Japanese side is more likely to be perfectionist, trying to discuss detailed matters from the start. Furthermore, one might remember that the current Indian management is conducted by a younger generation, with managers who are more culturally in tune with Western ones[3].

III. Bilateral Collaboration in Indian Infrastructure

(1) Japanese contribution to Indian infrastructure

It must be highlighted with respect to Japan–India economic relations that Japanese ODA has contributed greatly to improving Indian infrastructure. Not only was India the first recipient of Japanese ODA that was started in 1958; it has also been the largest recipient of Japanese ODA since 2003. Aside from making a dent in infrastructure development in India in the fields of power sector, transportation, and water supply and sewage, Japanese ODA has been instrumental in encouraging Japanese companies to invest into Indian infrastructure.

Japan has already left its footprint in Delhi Metro, which is credited for its punctuality and alleviating Delhi's severe traffic congestion, and also for the introduction of a new construction work culture: the concepts of "safety" and the "appointed time of delivery." Japan has already been committed to ODA metro railway projects not only in Delhi, but also in Kolkata, Bangalore, and Chennai. More Japan–India collaboration can be expected in future projects because fifty large cities with populations of more than two millions are expected to receive metro rail systems.

(2) Delhi–Mumbai Industrial Corridor

India has expressed its intention to construct five major Industrial Corridors[4] to drive India's growth in manufacturing and urbanisation. The five industrial corridors are Delhi–Mumbai, Amritsar–Delhi–

Kolkata, Chennai-Bengaluru, Bengaluru–Mumbai and Visakhapatnam–Chennai. Of those five industrial corridors, Japan is already committed to the Delhi–Mumbai Industrial Corridor (DMIC) and the Chennai–Bengaluru Industrial Corridor (CBIC). Civil engineering work on the DMIC project has already started.

The DMIC, with the Western Dedicated Freight Corridor (DFC) as its core backbone, is among the priority areas of Japanese sponsored investment into India, along with the CBIC in southern India. The vision of the DMIC is to build 24 industrial cities with world-class infrastructure across six states in Western India by 2040. Seven of them will be built for Phase 1 by 2019. The six states above are India's important commercial and industrial areas, accounting for 58 per cent of total industrial production, 45 per cent of total employment, and 57 per cent of total exports as on 2010. The project presents the possibility of the doubling of employment potential in seven years, tripling industrial output in nine years, and quadrupling of exports from the region in eight to nine years.

The idea of promoting the DMIC was endorsed at the Japan–India summit meeting in December 2006. It is an ambitious infrastructure project valued at US$ 90 billion, with financial and technical assistance from Japan. At the 2008 summit meeting, Japan pledged to provide a 450 billion yen loan to the first construction Phase 1 of the Western DFC. During the summit meeting in 2011, Japan pledged a US$ 4.5 billion loan to the DMIC project, including 18 prospective projects for constructing environmentally friendly smart communities including projects for power supply, railway (metro), and water supply. Among them, the logistics visualisation services project to bring efficiency in logistics and supply chain by affixing radio frequency identification (RfID) tags has started in 2016 as a joint venture between Japan's NEC Corp. and DMICDC (Delhi–Mumbai Industrial Corridor Development Corporation).

The Western DFC between Dadri in the National Capital Region (NCR) and Jawaharlal Nehru Port (JNPT) will be a safe and efficient transport system, spanning a distance of 1,462 km with a double line electric track. The DFC is expected to enhance freight transportation of bulk/heavy materials between Delhi and Mumbai to a great degree, and to reduce transportation times from three days to one day, while increasing freight volume per train by 3.7 times. Japanese companies play the role of prime contractors for each contract package under the Special Terms for Economic Partnership (STEP) loan[5]. After a long period of preparation, civil engineering work for Phase 1 (Rewari–Vadodra: 915 km) started in September 2013. Larsen and Toubro in tie-up with the Japanese trading company of Sojitsu as the prime contractor takes charge of the construction of railways because risk-averse Japanese major construction companies unanimously showed reluctance to bid for gigantic civil works projects under the Western DFC. Regarding the materials and equipment, rails are imported from Japan: head hardened rails to be made by Nippon Steel & Sumitomo Metal Co. Electric locomotives are going to be manufactured initially in Japan, but the production site will be transferred gradually to India. The Western DFC is scheduled to be opened partially in 2017 and entirely by 2020.

(3) Introduction of the Shinkansen System

The introduction of the Japan's high-speed railway (HSR) system, the so-called Shinkansen system to the Mumbai–Ahmedabad route is another landmark deal of Japan–India collaboration. According to the Ministry of Railway's Vision 2020, India has a plan to introduce high-speed trains to provide services at 250–350 km/h at six routes: Delhi–Amritsar, Pune–Mumbai–Ahmedabad, Hyderabad–Chennai, Howrah–Haldia, Chennai–Trivandrum, and Delhi–Patna. Of those six routes, the Mumbai–Ahmedabad route within the DMIC is the most promising from the standpoint of marketability, reflecting its high population density across the high-income region.

Japan has faced stiff competition from other countries in bidding for the project. This is reflected in the fact that a pre-feasibility study was conducted by a French company. Nevertheless, the Indian government places high confidence on the safety and punctuality of the Japan's HSR technologies. Following the summit meeting held in May 2013 between Prime Ministers Shinzo Abe and Manmohan Singh, the Memorandum of Understanding (MOU) was signed between Indian Railway and Japan International Cooperation Agency JICA) to conduct a joint feasibility study of the Ahmedabad–Mumbai route.

It was at the summit meeting held in Delhi in December 2015 that Prime Ministers Modi and Abe confirmed that the Shinkansen system would be introduced to the HSR on the Mumbai–Ahmedabad route[6], followed by the ceremony of laying cornerstone being taken place during the occasion of the summit meeting held in Gandhinagar in September 2017.

The Shinkansen system will sharply reduce the transportation time between Mumbai and Ahmedabad, spanning a 509 km from seven hours to two hours and 30 minutes. The total project cost for the Mumbai–Ahmedabad route will be INR 790 billion, where approximately 81 per cent of the total cost is to be covered by Japanese ODA[7]. According to the Memorandum of Cooperation signed by the Governments of Japan and India in December 2015, terms and conditions of loan are quite favourable for the Indian side: 0.1 per cent interest rate with a repayment of 50 years including moratorium for principle repayment for 15 years. It is unusual that such favourable terms and conditions of loan as indicated above would be applied to the Japanese ODA on such a large scale. The construction of HSR on the Mumbai–Ahmedabad route will be started in 2018. It will be completed by the end of 2023.

Human resources development for operation, maintenance and management of the HSR is indispensable for producing success in introducing the Shinkansen system to the Indian railway. As a matter of course, Japan is expected to play an important role in the training and uplifting of India's human resources in that area. As stipulated in the Memorandum of Cooperation described above, Japan and India are to be jointly engaged in training approximately 4,000 India's Ministry of Railway officials for operation of the HSR. Approximately 20 Indian officials are now being sent to Japan for study programme every year. The Japanese side is obligated to recruit around 150 professionals responsible for training Indian staff members. The most important information and know-how of the Shinkansen system are kept in hand completely by only two companies: East Japan Railway Company (JR East) and Tokai Japan Railway Company (JR Tokai). This time, JR East is totally assigned to the task of training as well as transfer of technologies of construction and manufacturing of HSR systems including rolling stock.

The introduction of the Shinkansen system to the Mumbai–Ahmedabad route will be financed on the basis of bilateral tied-loan, which means either only Japanese or Indian companies are entitled to play the role of prime contractors for each contract package. Different from the STEP loan, there is no mandatory requirement for procurement from Japan. As for the rolling stock of Shinkansen is concerned, the Japanese side is of opinion that considering security matters, the rolling stock should be manufactured in Japan at the initial stage, to be switched gradually to local production in India[8]. The challenges ahead include whether Japanese companies are willing to enter certain specific areas demanding high skills, such construction works as tunnels and viaducts, electrical networks, and railway sleepers, which are expected to be assigned to Japanese companies, and whether land acquisition can be accomplished smoothly. After the completion of construction, Japanese support will continue to be indispensable for the assurance of maintenance and operation. Win-win situations on the Shinkansen system will have the same impact as Maruti did on the automobile industry.

IV. Strategic and Global Partnership in a New Asian Era

(1) Formation of Strategic and Global Partnership

What makes Japan–India relations figure prominently among other bilateral relations in the Asian region that both Japan and India have gradually and steadily consolidated a bilateral framework for economic as well as security cooperation. As policy-makers appear to be convinced, an enduring bilateral relationship cannot be built unless it is underpinned by strategic ties (Naidu, 2004). Japan–India relations temporarily soured when India conducted nuclear tests in 1998, followed by Japan's freezing of grant aid (except for emergency, humanitarian and grassroots assistance) for new projects and suspending yen loans for new projects. It was Prime Minister Yoshiro Mori's visit to May 2000 that marked a starting point for the subsequent improvement of bilateral relations. The "Global Partnership between Japan and India" was launched, which confirmed that the two countries would work together by pooling their strengths and expertise not only for their mutual benefit, but for the rest of the world as well.

Prime Minister Junichiro Koizumi's visit to India in April 2005 marked the launch of the "Japan–India Partnership in a New Asian Era", which was aimed at reinforcing the strategic emphasis on the global partnership between the two countries against the background of geopolitical change in Asia triggered by China's assertive emergence. Japan succeeded in inviting India along with Australia and New Zealand as the founding members of the East Asian summit (EAS) when it was founded in December 2005. With a view to check a growing Chinese ascendancy in the EAS, Japan assigned more weight to the 'ASEAN+6' framework rather than the 'ASEAN+3' (Japan, China and Korea) framework as promulgated by China.

At the Tokyo summit meeting in December 2006, Prime Ministers Singh and Abe announced the "Joint Statement towards Japan–India Strategic and Global Partnership". The Joint Statement held great importance because it confirmed that both Prime Ministers would visit each other every other year. India was the first case for Japan to make an official promise of mutual visitation. For India it was the second case after Russia. Since then, along with the prime minister's mutual visitation, annual ministerial dialogues between their foreign ministries, defence ministries, and ministers dealing with finance, economy, trade, and energy have been institutionalised.

The "Joint Declaration on Security Cooperation between Japan–India" signed at the summit meeting in October 2008 is noteworthy for provided a comprehensive framework for enhanced security cooperation between the two countries. For India, this was the second security agreement after it signed with Australia in March 2007. It was followed up by the Action Plan in December 2009, which outlined more detailed strategic and defence cooperation, including annual strategic dialogue between foreign ministers, annual subcabinet/senior official 2+2 dialogue, and bilateral naval exercises.

The Japan–India annual summit meeting has been decisively important in implementing bilateral collaboration in Indian infrastructure. It is no exaggeration to say that such a gigantic project as DMIC/DFC project could not have taken shape or the final decision to introduce the Shinkansen system to the Mumbai–Ahmedabad would have been deferred without the framework of Strategic and Global Partnership.

(2) Bilateral Relations Keeping an Eye on the Indo-Pacific

Prime Minister Narendra Modi attaches no less great importance to relations with Japan than Mr. Manmohan Singh. Mr. Modi has a close personal bond with Prime Minister Mr. Shinzo Abe, viewing Japan as an "all-weather" friend, strategically committed to India's economic modernisation (Baru, 2016). Prime Ministers Abe and Modi adopted the "Tokyo Declaration for Indo–Japan Special Strategic and Global Partnership" in September 2014, elevating Japan and India's bilateral relationship to the Special Strategic and Global Partnership, stressing further progress in bilateral security and further expansion of Japanese investment into India. Both Japan and India set a target of doubling Japanese FDI and the number of companies. Japan expressed its intention to provide 3.3 trillion yen in public and private financing to India over the next five years.

As for the security partnership, both countries affirmed the importance of regular bilateral maritime exercises and Japan's continued participation in the India–US Malabar exercise series. They also decided to discuss elevation of the official trilateral dialogue between Japan, India, and the United States to a dialogue among their foreign ministers.

The "Japan and India Vision 2025 Special Strategic and Global Partnership" was announced at the Delhi summit meeting in December 2015, which showed further deepening of bilateral relations in the field of economic and security cooperation. Prime Ministers Abe and Modi welcomed the conclusion of the two security-related agreements related to the transfer of the defence equipment and technology, and related to security measures for the protection of classified military information. The agreements described above would make way for future projects on defence equipment and technology cooperation including Japanese US-2 amphibious aircraft, and would deepen bilateral defence cooperation for the defence of the SLOCs (Sea Line of Communications) in the Indo-Pacific region.

With regard to bilateral collaboration in infrastructure development, the two Prime Ministers confirmed that, in addition to the ongoing DMIC project, the Chennai Bengaluru Industrial Corridor (CBIC) project would be implemented using ODA loan schemes. It is noteworthy that in the field of railway, apart from the described above introduction of the Japanese Shinkansen system to the Mumbai–Ahmedabad route, the two Prime Ministers confirmed the signing of the memorandum of comprehensive technical cooperation including railway safety, rolling stock manufacturing, and station re-development, which would broaden commercial opportunities Japanese companies.

At the summit meeting held in Tokyo in November 2016, the Agreement for Cooperation in the peaceful Use of Nuclear Energy was signed, which would enable Japanese companies, including their subsidiaries in the United States, to export their nuclear plants to India. The two Prime Ministers decided to seek synergy between India's "Act East Policy" and Japan's "Free and Open Indo-Pacific Strategy" for better regional integration and improved connectivity as well as industrial networks, in which enhancing road connectivity in North East India and cooperation in the development of infrastructure and connectivity for the Iranian port of Chabahar were also mentioned. At the latest summit meeting held in Gandhinagar in September 2017, the Two Prime Ministers expressed their strong commitment to work together in India and with other countries in the Indo-Pacific region including Africa.

It was at the 2015 Delhi meeting that the Indo-Pacific concept was introduced for the first time at the summit meeting. The Indo-Pacific is a geographical terminology of a "broader Asia," which originated in a speech made by Prime Minister Abe (2007) at the Indian Parliament in 2007, under the title of "Confluence of the Two Seas". Subsequently, then Secretary of State Hillary Clinton (2011) noted the importance of translating the growing connection between the Indian and Pacific Oceans into an operational concept, indicating that the "stretch of sea from the Indian Ocean through the Strait of Malacca to the Pacific contains the world's most vibrant trade and energy routes." The Indo-Pacific concept reflects the fact that the accelerating economic and security connections between the Western Pacific and the Indian Ocean region are creating a single strategic system against the background of the geographically expanding interests and reach of China and India (Medcalf, 2016).

Recognising that peace, stability, and development in the Indo-Pacific are indispensable to their national security and prosperity, the "Japan and India Vision 2025" emphasised the importance of close cooperation between Japan and India which is the key to achieving peace and stability in the Indo-Pacific. The Indo-Pacific concept has also gone current among the United States, which is exemplified by the fact that President Donald Trump used the "Indo-Pacific," instead of the "Asia Pacific" at his remarks made at the Asian Pacific Economic Cooperation (APEC) Summit held in Da Nang in November 2017.

Prospects and Challenges

Japan and India have established a framework for long-term economic and security cooperation under the Strategic and Global Partnership. Both security and economic relations exerts a marked synergy effect on consolidating bilateral Japan–India relations as a whole. As Asia's leading democracies, both Japan and India share the belief that they will serve as key anchors for advancing peace, stability, and prosperity in Asia. The two countries have a mutual interest in dealing with an assertive China, a nation that has become the most important trading partner for each country.

The Modi government is strongly committed to enhancing infrastructure that Japan has already left a footprint upon. India regards Japan as a key partner to upgrade its manufacturing and infrastructure. As a matured economy with declining birth rates, Japan regards its strong partnership with India as important for its own growth scenario. Japanese corporate leaders harbour high expectations for Prime Minister Modi's leadership in improving the investment climate in India. The "Make in India" initiative under the Modi government provides further momentum for accelerating Japanese FDI and financing to India. The expansion of an East Asian supply chain that includes India is expected to provide both opportunities and challenges for Japanese companies investing into India.

India is now committed to many ambitious industrial corridor projects throughout the country. It is noted that with Japan is India's leading partner in building industrial corridors, high-speed railway and freight corridors, urban metro, as well as connectivity initiatives in India's North East (Delhi Policy Group, 2017). The integration of external and domestic corridors will engender the creation of a dynamic international production network linking South Asia to ASEAN and East Asia, with centre of gravity of the network gradually reaching India.

Under the banner of One Belt One Road Initiative (OBOR), China is now aggressively extending investment for building connectivity across Asia and Africa through both land and sea routes. China's infrastructure investment is intended for expanding Chinese influence and interests. In contrast, Japanese infrastructural development with ODA is characterised by people-centred investment, devoting attention to inclusiveness, resilience, and capacity building. Given that Japan and India share the values and commitment to the ideals of democracy, tolerance, pluralism, and an open society, it is highly important that both Japan and India promote their mutual cooperation and enhance connectivity among the Indo-Pacific area.

Notes

1. Data for Japanese FDI can be accessed at the Japan External Trade Organisation's (JETRO's) homepage, https://www.jetro.go.jp/world/japan/stats/fdi.html.
2. The Deming Prize, among the highest awards for TQM in the world, was established in 1991 by the Union of Japanese Scientists and Engineers (JUSE) in commemoration of the late Dr William Edwards Deming who contributed greatly to Japan's proliferation of statistical quality control after World War II. The total number of those companies awarded the Deming Prize has amounted to almost 240, most of which were Japanese companies. However, looking at the recent period of 2001–2016, of the total 61 awarded companies, as many as 26 companies were Indian companies.
3. India is ranked 3rd in the world with more than 4,200 start-ups. India is the youngest start-up nation in the world, with 72 per cent of the founders being younger than 35 years old (NASSOM, 2016).
4. If one connects the five industrial corridors, then they almost overlap with the highway network of the Golden Quadrilateral.

5. Conditions of STEP loans require that at least 30 per cent of Japanese funding be used for the import of equipment and goods from Japan. STEP loan offers more favourable terms of 0.1 per cent interest rate with 40 year repayment including 10 year grace period, compared with 1.4 per cent interest of general terms. A STEP loan is expected to raise the visibility of Japanese ODA in both recipient countries and Japan through the best use of advanced technologies and know-how of Japanese firms.
6. Japan was very anxious to reach an agreement on the Mumbai–Ahmedabad route all the more because Japan lost to China in the bidding of HSR in Indonesia in September 2015, just three months before the summit meeting.
7. The Japanese ODA (yen loan) will not cover import taxes, land acquisition costs and administration costs, or other ineligible costs and fees, as mutually agreed.
8. Personal interview with a senior official of JR East, conducted on 16 June 2016.

References

Abe, Shinzo (2007), "Confluence of the Two Seas", Speech at the Parliament of the Republic of India, 22 August, http://www.mofa.go.jp/region/asia-paci/pmv0708/ speech-2.html (accessed 17 August 2016).

Akamatsu, Kaname (1962), Historical Pattern of Economic Growth in Developing Countries", *Developing Economies*, Vol. 1.

Baru, Sanjaya (2016), "Two Years of the Narendra Modi Government in India—A View from Indian Perspective", *Gendai Indo Foramu (Contemporary India Forum)*, Summer No. 30.

Clinton, Hillary (2011), "America's Pacific Century", *Foreign Policy*," http://foreignpolicy.com/2011/10/11americas-pacific-century/ (accessed 17 August 2016).

Delhi Policy Group (2017), "India and Connectivity Frameworks", http://delhipolicygroup.org/uploads_dpg/publication_file/india-and-connectivity-frameworks-1074.pdf (accessed 27 November 2017)

Medcalf, Rory (2016), "Australia's New Strategic Geography", Priya Chacko (ed.) *New Regional Geopolitics in the Indo-Pacific: Drivers, Dynamics and Consequences* (London and New York: Routledge).

Naidu, G.V.C. (2004), "Whither the Look East Policy: India and Southeast Asia", *Strategic Analysis,* Vol. 28, No. 2, Apr–Jun 2004.

NASSCOM¶ 0SSCOM "National Association of Software and Services Companies0SSCOM", (2015) *The IT-BPM Sector in India: Strategic Review 2015* (New Delhi: NASSCOM).

———— (2016), *The IT-BPM Sector in India: Strategic Review 2016* (New Delhi: NASSCOM).

Chapter - 3

How Strategic is the Japan-India Partnership?

—Masanori Kondo

More than a 100 years ago, while delivering a lecture on "The Secret of Success" at the High Commerical College in Tokyo, Swami Ram Tirtha stressed on work, self-sacrifice, self-forgetfulness, universal love, cheerfulness, fearlessness and self-reliance.

The venerable Indian sage's suggestion to the students and teachers listening to him in rapt attention was to focus on "Come, Come" as differentiated from "Go, Go". As if on cue, more than a century later, India and Japan are still inviting each other to "Come, Come" so as to gain from each other's expertise in various fields.

The friendship between India and Japan is a work in progress that is moving in the right direction with co-operation ranging from automobiles and rail to nuclear energy and education. In August 2011, India and Japan signed a Comprehensive Economic Partnership Agreement.

In July 2017, the two countries also brought into effect, the India-Japan Agreement for Cooperation in the Peaceful Uses of Nuclear Energy. This was a great step forward because India's ever rising hunger for electricity can only be satiated with nuclear energy though as is the case with most things in South Asia - the roadblocks remain.

Since 2003, India is the biggest recipient of financing through the Japan International Cooperation Agency, or JICA, which is also described as the Japanese World Bank. Nearly a third of Japan's global financial assistance goes to India and this isn't surprising considering the country's size. Japan provides loans and other types of financial assistance to the tune of around INR 150-200 billion rupees annually to India - financing projects such as dams, hydroelectricity, waterways, ports, railways and highways.

India's contribution into the Japanese market is not significant. Most of Japanese needs for Information Technology come from the US. Similarly, India, an IT giant to boot, exports bulk of its services to US and Europe. Around 60 per cent-70 per cent of India's IT exports are to the US, 10 per cent to UK while Japan share has declined to one per cent- two per cent, down from three per cent earlier.

Corporates in Japan are gung-ho about India's economic prospects and believe that the country is now in a stage of recovery from the weak growth levels that it slumped into in the early part of this decade because of the spillover impact of the global financial crisis.

The Japanese investment into India will continue to grow but doing business in the country is not easy. The Japanese's manufacturing facilities in South East Asia and even some of the emerging markets are flourishing. These investments are driven by getting tax incentives, manageable labour and export opportunities and Japan wants India to emulate their example.

Under the current and the previous dispensation, India and Japan have a close working relationship. Investors in Japan are appreciative of India's desire to clean up the country of its "bad habits", particularly the widespread corruption.

Unfortunately, there haven't been any major reforms under the current Indian dispensation though small changes in policies were made.

The biggest reform so far an effort to punish the expropriators of black money has been the demonetisation of high value currency notes worth 500 and 1,000 rupees but it ended in dismal failure. It doesn't seem to have achieved the desired ends because most of the money returned into the system as those who had stashed away their ill-gotten wealth, managed to get it back into the mainstream channels of banking.

If the black money had not been legalised, or the hoarders of black money been apprehended with their hard cash and punished, the government would have scored a big victory. The failure of this policy is all the more tragic because demonetisation was a good political move with many among the public accepting it as an attempt to confront the hoarders of cash among the rich. Alas! it was not to be.

Demonetisation led to extensive suffering among the masses, not only those who were holding cash at home but the country at large. There was a cascading effect as many small and medium enterprises were unable to pay salaries to their employees who were rendered jobless. The working class or labourers who live on daily wages were also badly hit and with no cash at hand returned to their native villages from the big towns and metropolitan cities where they used to work. The local flourishing remittance economy, under which workers and employees transferred money to their near and dear ones from large cities to the mofussil areas, came to a standstill.

It goes without saying that the Japanese businesses view demonetisation as a disaster for consumers as it led to massive drop in prices. Prima-facie, lower prices seem to be good for the common man but in reality a sudden and significant drop eroded the earnings of businesses and their ability to pay their employees and workers. The daily wage earners and members of the middle class can't reap the benefits of lower prices, if their purchasing power is hit. Even if goods become cheaper, money is needed to purchase them, which is not available, if salaries are cut or there is retrenchment.

Price volatility, too high or too low prices, is not good for business. The Japanese were not affected directly by India's demonetisation but they monitored the adverse impact, which was mostly on the consumer goods sector but also on the home appliances division to a certain extent. Such a dire scenario cannot be dovetailed into any successful business strategy.

Policy Reforms

India had been trying to frame this uniform taxation policy through a Goods and Services Tax, or GST for a very long time.

Its implementation will reap positive results in the medium term but there will be initial pain to be borne out. The current government has finally implemented the GST regime, a logical culmination of the legacy of the previous governments, which took the lead in the first place. Now more needs to be done by a phased reduction of taxes.

Rather than increasing taxes, India should reduce government debt by cutting down on subsidies, while abolishing or slashing income tax.

India has promised to deregulate many industries so as to revitalise them. Plans include making it easy for small enterprises and foreign companies to enter new markets. Such industries include power generation, transportation, information technology, manufacturing, financing, agriculture and education. While baby steps have been taken in some areas but major reforms are yet to see the light of the day.

There are also risks that can make India's economic policy unsuccessful. These include potential opposition from political parties and conservative social groups. Unrealistically high expectations from the government can also lead to a severe backlash, even on minor setbacks. Adverse weather due to the El-Nino and La-Nina ocean currents have already resulted in a string of droughts and floods over the past few years and badly hurt India's farmers. A spate of suicides keep getting reported across the country. External risks include terrorism, a potential worsening of the situation in Iraq, rampant fluctuations in oil prices and changes in US financial policy.

While Japan is currently focusing more on macroeconomics and the financial industry, India is concentrating on micro sectors and governance.

India's government is making efforts to expand the scope of e-Governance which will hopefully improve the business environment. The businessmen in Japan believe it will take time for India to put in place governance procedures of international standards, as desired by investors from overseas. It is not the first time that a government in India is making economy a critical spoke of the administrative wheel. Ever since India unleashed the waves of economic liberalisation under thc then Finance Minister, Manmohan Singh, the country is on a roller coaster ride but almost three decades later, the task is far from complete.

It is still far more difficult to do business in India compared with Thailand, Malaysia, China, Indonesia and Singapore. There are problems related to administrative laws, labour, land and entrepreneurial partnerships.

India is notorious for shutting down factories for one reason or another. Bad experiences of the past include the shutting down of the Kolkata branch of Bank of Tokyo-Mitsubishi, closure of Mitsui's office in Mumbai due to legal problems and the labour strike at Maruti Suzuki factory in Manesar, near Gurugram. In July 2012, there were riots at the Manesar factory, a fire broke out, a section of the unit was gutted, an officer lost his life in a melee and 90 others were injured.

The Maruti strike was a massive headache and the henchmen didn't even bother to apologize over the issue and instead adopted a belligerent attitude. The car is made by Suzuki and sold through Maruti Suzuki. The seriousness of the situation can be gauged from the fact that a local court convicted 31 workers and gave life imprisonment to 13 among them.

One of the big moves made by India, exclusively eyeing investments from Japan is the setting up of Japan Plus. This is a single window facility set up to process investments from Japan in the Department of Industrial Policy and Promotion.

Japanese Projects in India

Japan's strength continues to be in the manufacturing sector. They are also active in Banking and Information Technology sectors but negotiating financial deals is the forte of a select group of agencies such as JICA.

A prime example of Japanese success stories in India is Maruti Suzuki. The joint venture has more than 50 per cent share in India's automobiles market. The manufacturers of car components, mostly Suzuki affiliates, have also had a good run in India's automobile industry.

Despite the bad experiences in Manesar and Gurugram, Maruti Suzuki is not moving out of Haryana. It sources ancillaries from the factory that its parent company, Suzuki has set up in Gujarat, which is more of an original equipment manufacturer, or OEM for Maruti. The parent company, Suzuki is a direct investor in the Gujarat unit and plans to double its car making capacity there and will also set up a facility there for manufacturing engines.

The aim is to have an annual capacity to produce more than two million units including close to a combined 1.6 million in the two factories in Haryana. The cars in Gujarat are manufactured by Suzuki and sold through Maruti Suzuki.

Hero Honda, which is also a joint venture between Indian and Japanese companies is another success story while Sony is making television sets.

Now time has come for Japan to focus on high-end automobile products and to move manufacturing to the most cost-effective production bases. Toyota, for one, has avoided making high-end cars in India. They are strong in the medium-end segment in India and believe that the dynamics of the country's market will change in the coming years with a wide range of business and policy reforms. Companies do not want to change strategies unless these reforms take place.

Toyota is, once again, expected to put its luxury brand cars in the Indian market by shipping them into the country. The likes of Lexus, will be exported from Thailand, where it already has a large facility for Asian markets.

Panasonic has recently appointed a top executive as in-charge for the Indian market. This is one good signal that the Japanese corporations are getting more serious about the Indian market. In the past, big corporate groups in Japan viewed the Indian market through the prism of relatively lower ranking executives.

One of the most important Japanese project in India pertains to the railways. Delhi Metro, which is now a household name with millions using it every year and a success story emulated in other parts of the country, would not have seen the light of the day without the financial help provided by Japan through JICA. The Mumbai-Ahmedabad rail projects involving Delhi may showcase Japanese technology for high speed trains. The trillion-yen, Mumbai-Ahmedabad bullet train project is being fast tracked for benefit of the public.

Japan provided the much needed financial support to kick-off the Delhi Metro project but coaches were imported from other countries such as South Korea, Spain, China and Germany. A section of the Japanese businesses feel Japan got a raw deal. Another perception that has gained ground is that most of the Japanese contractors who had tried to work on Indian projects didn't earn decent profits. Malaysian contractors have done well in India's highways sector while China is more likely to be exporting plants for power generation and South Korea relatively benefited more out of Metro train projects.

Japan is keen to see more Japanese rail projects in India but is facing a stiff competition from China whose company is doing a feasibility study of the Mumbai-Delhi high speed rail project.

China Railway Rolling Stock Corporation, or CRRC has secured a 69-coach supply contract for the Nagpur Metro in the province of Maharashtra. Nagpur is the headquarters of the Rashtriya Swyamsevak Sangh, or RSS, which is the ideological fountainhead and parent organisation of India's main ruling party, BJP, or Bharatiya Janta Party.

While Japan's government is keen on the country getting a larger pie in India's mass rapid transit and high speed rail projects but private companies beg to differ. Kawasaki, Hitachi and Toshiba are just not convinced about setting up rail-coach or related manufacturing facilities in India, citing land and labour-related issues as well as limited scope for exports of surplus units. Some favour the approach adopted in the Delhi Metro project with the company inviting global bids for various works while the funding was provided by JICA.

India is a massive consumers' market with an insatiable appetite for technology-driven products but exports from the country are just not competitive compared with shipments of the same product from facilities in other parts of the world with solid backing of tax-related incentives. All markets including Africa can be covered from

South East Asian facilities–automobiles from Thailand and television sets from Malaysia. The competition is cut-throat and even in the low-income markets of Africa, Japanese goods manufactured in Southeast Asia are out priced by South Korea and China. For a Japanese company to manufacture industrial goods in India and export to African countries will be a long haul, though there are exceptions such as Maruti Suzuki cars.

Kawasaki learnt an expensive lesson the hard way when it relocated a rail-facility to China. It is now financially bruised while competing with its Chinese counterparts in manufacturing coaches and other railway ancillaries for the export markets. China adopted Japan's rail-related technology and is now manufacturing engines, tracks, coaches and wagons at even lower costs. Private companies in Japan have apprehensions that India may follow suit if they set up manufacturing units there while they will be left saddled with costly infrastructure with limited demand.

Going Nuclear With Civility

Nuclear power for civilian use such as electricity generation is a win-win situation for both India and Japan. The two countries have already entered into a civil nuclear energy agreement.

While this is good news, the bad news is that Toshiba-Westinghouse has run into financial trouble and is facing bankruptcy and GE Hitachi is deeply conservative while considering moves to invest in India and start a nuclear energy plant.

As part of a historical legacy, Russia, with a greater risk taking appetite, is still investing in India's nuclear plants but in contrast the Japanese and the Americans are staying away and the reasons are not too far to seek.

India's law on civilian use of nuclear energy says if any accident happens, procurement and equipment supplier and not the operator will be held responsible and will be liable to pay compensation. The stringent law isn't surprising and has its origins in the horrifying Bhopal Gas Disaster of 1984. The culprit, Union Carbide didn't pay adequate compensation at the time or later and therefore India put in place this law, demanding compensation from equipment suppliers in the event of any future mishaps.

Nuclear energy companies refuse to play ball because if they invest in India and there is an accident, the compensation involved can lead to bankruptcy. It is too risky to start such greenfield projects though India insists that relevant insurance can be put in place to avoid an extreme case scenario.

The Japanese are aware of India's business like attitude when it comes to sourcing hardware supply, which incidentally comes cheaper from China. Price-wise China's power generators are 50 per cent cheaper compared with other global suppliers.

Japan's reading of China's business strategies is that it also wants to have a lion's share in India's renewable energy market. That said, there remains a trust deficit between the two giant Asian neighbours owing to China's steadfast refusal to allow Indian entry in the Nuclear Suppliers' Group, or NSG. The latest stand-off in Sikkim over China's surreptitious attempts to build a road and thereby capture territory at the disputed tri-junction with India and Bhutan hasn't helped matters either. It is geo-political issues such as these that give Japan an edge in the Indian market.

India and Japan face a common threat from a self-aggrandising China and are therefore comrade-in-arms. In 2015, Japan lifted its decades-long self-imposed ban on weapons exports.

The two countries have already been holding discussions at the ministerial level and will put even more focus on the issue of military co-operation. In an example related to security collaboration, Japan, India and the US have explored the potential of joint military exercises. India has decided to buy the ShinMaywa US-2 amphibious search and rescue aircraft for its navy from Japan and the two countries are trying to find a common ground on pricing.

Japan's Mitsubishi-Kawasaki Heavy Industries consortium is among the final shortlist of six manufacturers to have received a Request for Information from the Indian Navy for an eventual US$8 billion contract to build six advanced submarines with air-independent propulsion, or AIP technology, to stay submerged for longer duration and substantially increase their operational range.

In 1993, India began a "Look East" diplomacy policy - rejigged as "Act East" 20 years later - a strategy aimed at establishing amicable relationships with Southeast Asia amid the emergence of China as a major regional player. In 1998, India conducted successful tests of nuclear weapons but from 2000, it has become clear that India aims to become a superpower through economic growth.

India is working hard towards becoming a large maritime power. To achieve the goal, India will probably cooperate even more with the US and strengthen its Act East policy, politically and economically, specially with Vietnam, Singapore and Japan.

In the meantime, China has set its ambitions sky high but it may end up in deep morass by framing plans for a US$900 billion land and maritime silkroad initiative for the twenty-first century. It may be in for an unpleasant surprise because things are not as smooth as silk. The project is not commercially viable at all and China will lose money on it.

Another Chinese initiative, the Asian Infrastructure Investment Bank, or AIIB, that started operations in December 2015, is doing better compared with the Silk Road initiative and its lending pattern is being closely tracked by international investors and other funding agencies. Being a China-led international financial institution created in the same year and with the same purpose, it may give top priority to finance infrastructure projects that are part of the Silk Road initiative.

India's major problem with the Silk Road is that by far its most critical component, the China-Pakistan Economic Corridor, passes through disputed areas that are claimed by both India and Pakistan and are currently in control of the latter and by proxy-of China. China has an obsession with constructing roads in disputed areas, which can then be used for deployment of the armed forces.

However, war will not be to the benefit of any of these key players in the Eastern theater and all countries realise this only too well to go for the jugular.

Instead, the shrewd mandarins in Beijing are currently focused on only three things-markets, markets and more markets, while New Delhi accepts the reality that border disputes are the stuff long drawn out negotiations are made of and is instead looking at bridging the bilateral trade deficit with China.

As the then premiers Manmohan Singh and Wen Jiabao had once remarked, world has enough space for the growth ambitions of both India and China. One can also add Japan to this matrix.

Chapter - 4

New Delhi-Tokyo Axis: Towards a 'New' Regional Order in Asia

—Netajee Abhinandan

India, in recent times, has been assiduously trying to redefine its role in Asia as well as global political system. There have been new (foreign) policy formulations and recalibration of old policies in order to adjust effectively to the ever-changing power relations, both at the regional and global level, and also the emerging world order. The shift in India's approach is most apparent in its stance towards the countries in the 'extended neighbourhood'-in Southeast, Central and West Asia and also Indo-Pacific region- as it strives hard to reach out to these regions for achieving greater economic and strategic leverage in Asia. There has been great effort, of late, by the present government to revitalise relations with those countries and regions which were previously not part of India's foreign policy priorities. The pronouncements such as 'Act East', 'Connect Central Asia', 'Look West' and 'Project Mausam' underline the importance India attaches to building strong partnerships with the countries in these regions. Prime Minister Narendra Modi, particularly, has taken keen interest to intensify India's engagement with the countries in India's extended neighbourhood which largely remained at the margins of foreign policy agenda. The emerging patterns of India's external engagement strategy under Modi government signify three broad goals–strengthening its regional position in Asia and thereby counter the hegemonic influence of China, playing a proactive role in world affairs by becoming a part of the global political and economic architecture and finally intensifying the process of economic modernisation in the country through vital support from different countries. All these three objectives are inter-connected and contribute to the larger vision of India aspiring to achieve greater global strategic influence. There is a realisation that India can never achieve high economic growth just by concentrating on domestic reforms and initiatives. Modi understands that for India to achieve its goals it has to deepen its engagement with various countries- in immediate and extended neighbourhood and all major powers- seeking investment, technology and expertise. The subtle, yet significant, shift in India's foreign policy priorities can also be seen as a response to the dynamics of changing power relation in Asia. In this context, India's efforts to strengthen its partnership with Japan assume significance.

India and Japan: The Move towards Greater Engagement

Since the new government took over under the leadership of Prime Minister Narendra Modi, there has been special focus on deepening ties with Japan and take the relations forward to the level of strong strategic partnership that would be long-term and mutually beneficial. While Modi inherited strong India-Japan relations from the previous governments, the back to back visits of Modi and Japan Prime Minister Shinzo Abe have certainly helped in creating a personal chemistry between the two 'charismatic' leaders and elevating the relations to a Special Strategic and Global Partnership, underscoring the growing bonhomie. The beginning of a new phase of understanding between the countries can be traced to 2007 when both the sides concluded a strategic agreement. A joint declaration of New Delhi and Tokyo announced that this accord would become an "essential pillar for the future architecture" of Asia. Since then, the two countries have signed a comprehensive economic partnership agreement and have held talks on a potential civil nuclear deal. It must be noted that Modi's special bonding with Japan can be traced to his days as the Chief Minister of Gujarat when he embarked on cultivating a strong bond with Japan External Trade Organisation (JETRO) while attracting investments to the state.[1]

Modi's first visit to Japan as Prime Minister in September 2014, in many ways, can be considered as a turning point "cementing Asia's new democratic axis and co-opting Tokyo as an important partner in India's development and a collaborator on mutual security."[2] He was largely successful in creating renewed interest among the Japanese investors for doing business in India by pledging to curb red-tapism and promising to open a Special Management Team under the PMO to expeditiously facilitate Japanese investment projects. Harping on 3D's- democracy, demography and demand, Modi promoted 'Brand India'; marketing India as a manufacturing hub with huge potential for growth.[3] "Some people say there is thick red tape in India, but I would like you to believe there is a red carpet in India," he told Japanese businessmen.[4] During this visit, both the sides signed five pacts covering defence exchanges, cooperation in clean energy, roads and highways, healthcare and women while vowing to take their relationship from strategic partnership to a special strategic partnership. They also signed a MoU for cooperation in heritage conservation, city modernisation and cooperation in the fields of art, culture and academics. Signalling a greater appreciation of India's strategic interests, Japan lifted the ban on six Indian entities including Hindustan Aeronautics Limited (HAL) which was imposed in the aftermath of 1998 nuclear tests.[5] However, the biggest take away from this visit was Japan's commitment to invest $35 billion, through public and private funding, over a period of five years for developmental projects, including building of smart cities and cleanup of river Ganges. The proposed investment was a clear attempt by the Japanese leadership to provide fillip to economic relations, that was somewhat losing steam in recent years compared to its trade with China (US$311.995 billion in 2013), as Japan is vying for having greater access to alternate markets like India.

Japan Prime Minister Shinjo Abe's reciprocal visit to India in December 2015 further strengthened the ties. During this visit, both sides issued a futuristic blueprint titled 'Japan-India Vision 2025 Special Strategic and Global Partnership' outlining a roadmap for expanding the strategic partnership. In this document, Abe and Modi agreed on expanding bilateral cooperation in a wide range of issues from investment, disaster risk management, and people-to-people exchange. They also acknowledged that stability of the Indo-Pacific region to be 'indispensable' to their respective national security and prosperity, calling for a more robust cooperation in security issues. While during Modi's visit to Japan the focus was on boosting the economic and trade relations, Abe's India visit focused upon intensifying the strategic relations. In this context, it is noteworthy that after returning to power in December 2012, Abe penned an important commentary in which he introduced the 'Diamond Concept' (*daiyamondo kousou*), that envisaged an alliance among the United States, Japan, Australia, and India, forming a virtual security 'diamond' and working together to maintain the peace and stability of the Indo-Pacific region.[6] This doctrine got a boost when Japan and India signed two important security agreements. One was Japan-India agreement on defence equipment and technology transfer. This agreement paved the way for robust Japan-India cooperation in the area of defence technology as it entailed the establishment of a Japan-India Joint Committee for the oversight and prohibition of third-party transfers without prior approval. The other was the Agreement Concerning the Security Measures for the Protection of Classified Military Information. This agreement, commonly referred to as the general security of military information agreement (GSOMIA), obligated both Japan and India to protect classified military information exchanged between the two countries, thereby facilitating more robust intelligence exchanges between the Indian Armed Forces and the Japan Self-Defence Force (JSDF).[7]

Most significantly, both sides signed the "Agreement for Cooperation in the Peaceful Uses of Nuclear Energy" and a supplementary document, called "Note on Views and Understanding," also legally binding, to ensure the implementation of the main deal during Prime Minister Modi's visit to Japan in November 2016. This deal made India the first non-NPT signatory to ink a nuclear pact with Japan paving the way for a robust clean energy partnership. Emphasising the importance of the agreement, Modi said, "the memorandum on civil nuclear energy cooperation is more than just an agreement for commerce and clean energy. It is (a) shining symbol of a new level of mutual confidence and strategic partnership". The Joint Statement, issued on this occasion, indicated the intention of both governments to sign a bilateral agreement on joint participation in nuclear projects once "some technical details, including those that have to comply with international procedures" were reconciled.[8] The substantive statement not only delineated on issues of mutual interest but on Indo-Pacific regional issues as well signifying "the tectonic shift in India-Japan relationship in four areas: nuclear cooperation, counterterrorism, coordination on regional issues, and defence industry cooperation."[9] Japan, for the first time, came out openly in support of India urging Pakistan to take stringent measures against terrorist outfits operating from its soil. It was a major diplomatic breakthrough for India.

Apart from the civil nuclear agreement, nine other Memorandums of Understanding (MoUs) and Memorandums of Cooperation (MoCs) were also signed during Modi's visit. While the 'Manufacturing Skill Transfer Promotion Programme' (aimed at furthering 'Make in India' and 'Skill India') intended to provide skilled training to 30,000 strong workforce and establish of Japan-India Institute for Manufacturing (JIM) in three states, the MoU between Indian Space Research Organisation (ISRO) and Japan Aerospace Exploration Agency (JAXA) aimed to strengthen the bilateral cooperation, identify and carry out mutually beneficial cooperative projects on space applications, space exploration, research and development and promotion of the space industry. Agreement were also inked for collaboration in data sharing, joint research in marine and earth sciences as well as in the fields of agriculture and food industries, promoting investment in infrastructure projects in India, and improving the quality of Indian textiles for the Japanese market.

As part of Annual Bilateral Meet, Prime Minister Abe's September 2017 visit to India elevated the relations to a new level with both sides committing to strengthen their partnership in economic and strategic spheres and together play a more proactive role in the Indo-Pacific region. While the focus was clearly on the flagship multi-billion dollar Mumbai-Ahmedabad High Speed Rail Project, financed by Japanese credit of US$ 17 billion at a nominal 0.1 per cent interest rate, there were many other important takeaways from the Twelfth Indo-Japan Summit. Abe's visit happened in the midst of growing tension between India and China on the issue of control over Bhutan's Doklam plateau and North Korea's threats questioning the efficacy of

US' role as the global security guarantor. In this context, India and Japan are keen to join hands and play a strategic role countering China's hegemonic assertions and promoting rule-based diplomacy. Significantly, the joint statement called for "a free, open and prosperous Indo-Pacific region where sovereignty and international law are respected, and differences are resolved through dialogue, and where all countries, large or small, enjoy freedom of navigation and over flight, sustainable development, and a free, fair, and open trade and investment system." It also backed India's position on boycotting China's One Belt, One Road Initiative (OBOR). The joint statement, unlike previous versions, minced no words in condemning North Korea and Pakistan as trouble-makers in the region and pointed towards China's role in supporting them. It did well to portray India and Japan as democratic stabilisers challenging the Rawalpindi-Beijing-Pyongyang axis.

India-Japan Bonhomie: The China Factor

The rapidly growing relations between India and Japan have not only bilateral implications, but have implications for regional political order in Asia also, especially in the context of South China Sea dispute and increasing hegemonic influence of China. In recent times, the rapidly growing economic, political and military power of China has made many countries, including Japan, anxious, prompting them to invite other major external powers to engage in the region. Many believe that their political and strategic interests would be adversely affected with the rise of powerful China and its assertions over maritime resources in the region. These concerns have led to the promotion of the concepts of 'Asia-Pacific' and 'Indo-Pacific', which is evident with the US pivot to Asia and the direct mention and discussion in Australia's Defence White Paper (2013).[10] In this context, the efforts of both Modi and Abe to forge a strong strategic partnership have to be analysed. Apparently, the personal chemistry between the two leaders have contributed significantly to the evolving relations as they attempt to expand the manoeuvring space for themselves in Asia and thereby contain the Chinese influence. "Modi and Abe, whose personal ties date back to 2007, are both seen as conservative nationalists seeking to overhaul their economies and strengthen their militaries. Japan offers deep pockets, and India presents a growing market with a population set to overtake China as the world's largest in 2022."[11] While Abe is trying to bring Japan out of self-imposed Pacifism by empowering the Self-Defence Forces, Modi is investing more than $60 billion in India's navy to deter China from establishing a foothold in the Indian Ocean.[12] Modi, emphasising the importance of relations with Japan, said at a joint press conference with Abe at New Delhi, "I cannot think of a strategic partnership that can exercise a more profound influence on shaping the course of Asia and our interlinked ocean regions more than ours".[13]

With all the major powers including the US and South East Asian countries getting involved, South China Sea dispute has emerged as the most contentious issue affecting the power dynamics of Asia. On one side is China which claims sole control over the marine resources of South China Sea, on the other side are countries like Japan, Vietnam and the Philippines who challenge Chinese assertions and activities. Indo-Japanese maritime cooperation, in this context, becomes increasingly important. While India relies on continuous access to sea lines of communications (SLOCs) plying the Western Pacific waters for the commercial and trade transactions, Japan is dependent for its energy needs on the same access to SLOCs through the Indian Ocean Region. SLOC security therefore constitutes a key driver of this Indo-Japanese nexus in the maritime domain. China has sparred with Japan over the Senkaku Islands in the East China Sea, and India is concerned over Chinese moves to send submarines to Sri Lanka and build a port at Pakistan. Significantly, Modi and Abe called for a "peaceful, open, equitable, stable and rule-based order in the Indo-Pacific region and beyond" in their joint statement. It specified regular participation of Japanese navy in the large-scale American-Indian naval military exercise MALABAR that has been annually conducted in Bay of Bengal (the Indian Ocean) since 2007. In addition, the document stated the mutual agreement on holding "dialogues and joint events" in the tripartite format with the participation of the US. Japan agreed to help finance infrastructure projects in India, including roads in its north-eastern states, one of which is the disputed area of Arunachal Pradesh. In recent months, India has pushed ahead with plans to build a $6 billion highway and populate the remote region it has neglected since fighting a war over it with China five decades ago.[14]

Another area of concern for India and Japan is the ambitious projects like '21st Century Maritime Silk Road' (MSR) and 'One Belt One Road'(OBOR) being pushed vigorously by China to expand its power and influence across Asia, Europe and Africa through financing huge infrastructural projects. The much hyped project is part of China's attempts to establish multiple lines of communication that would link different regions of Asia to its economic heartland in eastern China. The underlying aim of such a geo-strategy is to develop inner Chinese provinces and shape China's regional periphery by exercising economic, political and cultural influence. It is a well-calibrated strategic initiative by China to not only enhance investment and foster collaboration across the historic Silk Road but also expand its sphere of influence beyond Asia. China maintains that MSR along with OBOR would increase connectivity among countries of Asia, Europe and Africa and would lead to trade flows and spur long-term regional economic growth and development, benefiting all those involved. This project aims to reinforce China's pre-eminence in Asia and establish a new sphere of influence, a modern-day version of the nineteenth century Great Game, where Britain and Russia battled for control in Central Asia.[15] It would also serve China's foreign policy goals in the Asia-Pacific region. While encouraging its neighbouring states to cooperate in the economic field without any political strings attached, Beijing has continued to assert its claims over the South China Sea, by transforming reefs and other submarine maritime features into fully operative islands complete with 3000 m runways, air defence installations etc.[16] The Maritime Silk Road also intends to intensify Beijing's partnership with friendly countries, such as Pakistan, Sri Lanka, Cambodia, and Malaysia. This, according to William Yale, an American expert, will be accomplished primarily by way of economic incentives, such as infrastructural development and trade agreements. China's Maritime Silk Road and its infrastructure investments and projects also aim to facilitate more frequent People's Liberation Army Navy (PLAN) deployments in the Indian Ocean and beyond. The PLAN requires reliable logistics chains across the Sea Lines of Communication (SLOC) throughout Southeast and South Asia.[17]

As per estimates, China will invest around $1.25 trillion abroad by 2025. Thus, China has drawn attention and enthusiasm from a vast geographic area, stretching across Eurasia, from the Far East and Central Asia, to the Middle East and Africa, and across the Western Pacific to Latin America, where China has made infrastructure investments, provided loans, and focused on commercial ties with nations such as Argentina, Brazil, Ecuador and Venezuela. Apart from the proposed Economic Corridor in Pakistan, China is working to develop other economic corridors with Central Asia and Europe, as evidenced by its newly opened landmark railway that links the Iberian Peninsula to China. While several infrastructural projects are ongoing in Africa, China proposes financing new projects in other continents, such as a Eurasian-North American transcontinental railway system that connects China, Russia, Canada and America via the Bering Strait. China is also in the process of developing a mega waterway project to link the Pacific and Atlantic through a new shipping canal across Nicaragua. Although China is not an Arctic nation, Chinese news sources have reported that China's Jilin province may be involved in opening a new ocean route passing from the North Pacific Ocean island of Sakhalin, the Kamchatka Peninsula, Bering Strait, and Arctic Ocean to reach Norway, the United Kingdom, the Netherlands, and other European countries.[18] Overall, these projects and proposals under the B&R initiative would help China in exercising soft-power diplomacy and economic influence that in turn strengthen its position as a dominant actor in global political system and thereby counter the growing influence of countries like India and Japan.

India is not totally convinced about the rationale, as put forward by China, behind such a humongous infrastructural imitative as it is constrained to believe that the MSR is basically a geo-strategic design to help China consolidate its naval / maritime strategy of access and basing in the Indian Ocean in support of PLA Navy's future operations. It is a ploy to dismiss the notion of 'string of pearls' strategy, dispel the 'China threat' in the Indian Ocean, and legitimize its engagement in various maritime infrastructure projects along the route.[19] India is concerned as China, under the B&R initiative, is developing ports in Bangladesh, Sri Lanka and Pakistan, and is trying to enlarge its sphere of influence using its economic might in the Bay of Bengal and

Arabian Sea. To counter Chinese plans, India and Japan are keen to work together to build a trade corridor of their own, linking India and other South East Asian countries with Africa. Prime Minister Narendra Modi proposed to start Asia-Africa Growth Corridor (AAGC) at a meeting of Asian Development Bank (ADB) in May 2017. The proposal was followed by the formal presentation of the 'vision document' for the project by the governments of India and Japan. Through this project, both the countries aim to curtail Chinese investments in Africa by providing an alternative platform. The AAGC plans to establish links between the two continents through connecting ports such as those in Jamnagar (Gujarat) with Djibouti in the Gulf of Eden, ports of Mombasa and Zanzibar to those near Madurai, and Kolkata with Sittwe port in Myanmar. The objective stated in the vision document talks about "creating a free and open Indo-Pacific region by rediscovering ancient sea-routes and creating new sea corridors." The project proposes to establish a series of enhanced, mostly sea-based economic triangles which will connect cities and other production hubs across regions that are expected to develop rapidly in near future focussing on areas of agriculture, health, technology, and disaster management. Most importantly, the AAGC, contrary to OBOR, intends to have consultation with all the stakeholders while carrying out the projects stressing on strong local ownership by African countries of projects under the corridor.

Japan, already working with India to build infrastructure in Iran, has committed to help India in building road and infrastructure projects in the North-East states and thus establish greater connectivity with countries like Myanmar and ASEAN countries. Already, Japan International Cooperation Agency (JICA) has signed an agreement with Indian government to provide over 67 billion yen (US$610 million) for Phase I of the North East Road Network Connectivity Improvement Project, which will be used for the implementation of important projects in states of Meghalaya and Mi-joram. For the AAGC project also, Japan has assured to provide bulk of financial support and work in tandem with India to expedite trans-continental connectivity and development projects. China, wary of Indo-Japan initiatives, has cautioned them not to disturb its OBOR in any way. A report in state-run *Global Times* said:

If India and Japan design the corridor to deliberately counterbalance China's OBOR, they should think twice before rushing to it because the route of the AAGC has an extensive geographic overlap with the route of the OBOR initiative. That's particularly the case, considering that China has already made huge commitments to developing Africa while the India-Japan partnership is only just taking shape.[20]

The Road Ahead

India realises that only through active collaboration with Japan, it can thwart the emergence of a Sino-centric Asia and safeguard its own strategic interests. Asia's balance of power will be largely determined by events in two key regions: East Asia and the Indian Ocean. "According to the 'Tokyo Declaration for India-Japan Special Strategic and Global Partnership' unveiled during Modi's visit, these two leading maritime democracies in Asia have agreed to 'upgrade and strengthen' their defence relations and work together on advancing security in Asia and the wider Indo-Pacific region, marked by the confluence of the Indian and Pacific Oceans."[21] The Declaration also affirmed the shared commitment of both the countries to maintain security over maritime resources, freedom of navigation and over flight, civil aviation safety, unimpeded lawful commerce, and peaceful settlement of disputes in accordance with international law. It was clearly a signal to China. The new Indo-Japanese axis, though evolving, is centred on a mutual recognition that such a coalition can potentially shape Asian geopolitics in much the same way as China's rise or America's 'pivot' to Asia.[22] China's emergence as a global power, relative decline in America's power and its gradual withdrawal from global crises have necessitated realignment of power relations both regionally and globally. At this juncture, Abe's re-election augurs well for both the countries as they seek to strengthen their partnership as strategic allies and rebalance the regional order in Asia. India and Japan, through concerted and coordinated efforts, can surely counter China's expansionist policies and challenge its territorial and maritime claims. The partnership, mutually beneficial, might shape new power equilibrium in Asia, changing the contours of existing power relationships.

References

1. Titli Basu, "India-Japan Relations: New Times, Renewed Expectations", IDSA Commentary, available at http://www.idsa.in/idsacomments/IndiaJapanRelations_tbasu_040914.
2. Brahma Chellany, " Why Modi's Japan Visit was a Watershed", available at http://www.rediff.com/news/column/brahma-chellaney-why-modis-japan-visit-was-a-watershed/20140903.htm.
3. Titli Basu, *op.cit.*
4. "Modi rolls out 'red carpet' for Japanese manufacturers", *Nikkei Asian Review*, September 2, 2014, available at http://asia.nikkei.com/Politics-Economy/International-Relations/Modi-rolls-out-red-carpet-for-Japanese-manufacturers.
5. "10 highlights of Modi's visit to Japan", *India Today*, September 3, 2014.
6. Yuki Tatsumi, "Abe's Visit Takes Japan-India Security Relations to the Next Level", *The Diplomat*, December 14,2015 available at http://thediplomat.com/2015/12/abes-visit-takes-japan-india-security-relations-to-the-next-level/.
7. *Ibid.*
8. Joint Statement issued during the visit of Prime Minister Shinzo Abe of Japan to India in New Delhi, December 12, 2015, Ministry of External Affairs, Government of India, December 12, 2015, athttp://www.mea.gov.in/bilateral-documents.htm?dtl/26177/List_of_document.
9. Prakash Paneerselvam, "Modi's Trip to Tokyo: Takeaways for India-Japan Relations", The Diplomat, at https://thediplomat.com/2016/11/modis-trip-to-tokyo-takeaways-for-india-japan-relations/
10. Government of Australia (2013), *Defence White Paper*, available at http://www.defence.gov.au/whitepaper2013/docs/WP_2013_web.pdf.
11. Natalie Obiko Pearson, "Abe-Modi deals shows Asia's top powers moving to keep rising China in check", *Japan Times*, December 14, 2015, available at http://www.japantimes.co.jp/news/2015/12/14/national/politics-diplomacy/japan-picked-china-build-indias-high-speed-rail-link-15-billion-deal/#.VsYCS_l97IX.
12. *Ibid.*
13. Media Statement by Prime Minister with Japanese Prime Minister in New Delhi (December 12, 2015), Press Information Bureau, Government of India, Prime Minister's Office, available athttp://pib.nic.in/newsite/PrintRelease.aspx?relid=133117.
14. Satoru Nagao and Koh Swee Lean Collin, "A Japan-Singapore-India Maritime Partnership", *The Diplomat*, February 12, 2016, available at http://thediplomat.com/2016/02/a-japan-singapore-india-maritime-partnership/

15. Charles Clover and Lucy Hornby, "China's Great Game: Road to a new empire", *The Big Read*, at http://www.ft.com/cms/s/2/6e098274-587a-11e5-a28b-50226830d644.html#axzz4H796g9Pz.
16. William Yale, China's Maritime Silk Road Gamble, *The Diplomat*, April 22, 2015, at http://thediplomat.com/2015/04/chinas-maritime-silk-road-gambl.
17. *Ibid.*
18. Yasemin Dobra-Manço, "China's Foreign Policy and Silk Road Initiatives Spur Cultural Diplomacy", at http://silkroutes.net/OBORChina Silk Road Routes Revival.htm.
19. Vijay Sakhuja, "Xi Jinping and the Maritime Silk Road: The Indian Dilemma", IPCS, at http://www.ipcs.org/article/china/xi-jinping-and-the-maritime-silk-road-the-indian-dilemma-4662.html.
20. "India-Japan growth corridor may mean division, not connectivity for Asia, Africa", *Global Times*, 1 August, 2017, at http://www.globaltimes.cn/content/1059129.shtml
21. Brahma Chellany, op.cit.
22. *Ibid.*

Chapter - 5

India-Japan Relations: New Beginnings in Strategic Symmetry?

—*Raviprasad Narayanan**

Introduction

For several decades, Japan and India had engaged in a process of bilateral diplomacy characterised by a sense of guarded scepticism bordering on mutual wariness. The early decades of India's external engagements since its independence in 1947 were marked by adopting and articulating a foreign policy of non-alignment in a post war world where bloc rivalry had polarised international relations. Tokyo's firm anchor in the western bloc and New Delhi's moral hectoring drove a weariness into the bilateral which until the turn of the century was somnolent. If there was a bilateral engagement between established democracies in Asia that had fallen short of expectations, it was undoubtedly that between Tokyo and New Delhi.

That sobering assessment is now giving way to a renewed push on both sides to correct decades long drift and arrive at a mutually satisfactory relationship where economic connectivity and strategic congruence merge into a real bilateral with institutional heft not encumbered by the shibboleths of the past. In other words, the form and substance of the bilateral engagement between the two countries were for long divergent with very little common ground, if any. If current trends are to be seen as a bilateral systemic shift in the making, we are witnessing an epochal moment in geopolitics with India and Japan beginning a strategic symmetry.

Recent developments especially over the past decade, have brought in a sense of excitement to the Japan-India bilateral and this article analyses the factors driving Tokyo and New Delhi closer and adopts a tone of critical evaluation into the causes and effects of this ongoing process.

Beginning anew

In May 1998, India tested nuclear devices leading to global opprobrium and perhaps the shrillest voice criticising the nuclear tests was from Japan. India's nuclear tests at Pokharan invited economic sanctions from Japan and the freezing of loans and grants with the only exception being humanitarian aid.

In a visible and most remarkable turnaround, Japanese prime minister Yoshiro Mori's visit to India in August 2000 turned a new definitive page in bilateral relations. Prime Minister Mori visited New Delhi and called India and Japan "global partners," a phrase previously reserved for the United States. It was during the Bharatiya Janata Party's (BJP) stewardship led by prime minister Atal Behari Vajpayee that the Mori visit witnessed establishment of a "Global Partnership between Japan and India." Moving beyond this, in April 2005, Japanese prime minister Junichiro Koizumi's visit began Japan-India annual summit meetings.

During the term of the Congress led United Progressive Alliance (UPA) led by prime minister Manmohan Singh, bilateral relations between the two countries was elevated to the "Global and Strategic Partnership" in 2006. Slightly less than a decade later, in 2014, with the BJP in power, bilateral relations between the two countries were elevated to "Global and Strategic Partnership."

Elevating the bilateral further was Japanese prime minister Shinzo Abe's visit to India in December 2015, where in sync with his host, prime minister Narendra Modi, the two countries decided to transform the bilateral global and strategic partnership into a deep, broad-based and action oriented partnership which brings together long-term political, economic and strategic goals. The "Japan and India Vision 2025 Special Strategic and Global Partnership Working Together for Peace and Prosperity of the Indo-Pacific Region and the World" is a joint statement laying out the contours of a relationship marking and highlighting Japan-India bilateral relations. In his reciprocal visit, in November 2016, prime minister Modi's summit with prime minister Abe witnessed the two sides wanting to lead the Indo-Pacific region through an era of prosperity and stability and coordinate over issues of common import.[1]

What are the motivating variables and determinants driving this growing and intensive congruence between Japan and India? And, what are the 'takeaways' dictating this coalescing of views?

This essay attempts to tease out the consistencies and inconsistencies in the bilateral.

(I) Analysing the bilateral 'ups' and 'downs'

A close reading of the diplomatic semantics between the two sides reveals a complete turnaround in Tokyo's evaluation of India. From a nadir in 1998, when India's nuclear tests led to global opprobrium, especially from Japan, the Mori visit in 2000 initiated the beginnings of a new engagement driven by domestic and external factors with growing commonalities actively encouraging the two sides to harmonise their views. A congruence of views is taking place with both countries taking steps to address erstwhile misgivings and replacing the same with a commitment that will stand the test of time, since both countries display a behavioural pattern shorn of aggression and a scrupulous abiding of established international norms. In other words, they are two actors sharing normative values, subscribing to an order where constructive cooperation makes for a predictable pattern of state behaviour, not shrill rhetoric. This section analyses the strategic, economic and political aspects to the bilateral.

(a) Strategic

In October 2008, India and Japan, represented by their prime ministers signed the India-Japan Joint Security Declaration, strongly underlining the bilateral as "an essential pillar for the future architecture of the region."[2]

Beyond bilateral agreements,what characterises Japan and India relations, is their steadfast adherence to democracy. It is this temperament that guides the two countries as they face challenges in the Indo-Pacific region. Democracies have a methodology in conducting diplomatic relations by initiating structural constructs in the form of multilateral institutions and relying on 'soft power' to advertise and extoll a temperament that speaks the language of cooperation.

The strategic determinant emerges, as the two countries acknowledge with wariness, the growing power and heft of China in the region. China's increasing centrality to power politics in the Asia-Pacific region comes at the expense of established norms in the region and a belligerent posture adopted by Beijing for rallying domestic nationalism. Japan has borne the brunt of this orchestrated version of stoking domestic nationalism by China, when infringements take place in the East China Sea especially the Senkaku islands, where Japan's sovereignty is challenged by China's 'historical' claims. China's laudable economic growth is accompanied by assertive actions in the maritime domain that encourages Japan to look for allies beyond the United States. This is precisely where India enters the picture. The United States remains Japan's security guarantor, yet, recent policy drift in Washington in matters of domestic and international, encourage doubt as to the commitment shown by Washington in staying the course in the Asia-Pacific, thereby creating a security vacuum being filled in by China, and its playing the 'victim' card of history. Importantly, furthering strategic linkages is the Indian Navy's 'Malabar' exercises where Japan's regular participation is much appreciated by India. Security linkages between the two sides has also seen the entry into force of the 'Defence Framework Agreement concerning the Transfer of Defence Equipment and Technology' and 'Security Measures for the Protection of Classified Military Information.' These agreements complement and add to the security and defence dialogue frameworks between Japan and India including the "2+2" Dialogue, Defence Policy Dialogue, Military-to-Military Talks and Coast Guard-to-Coast Guard cooperation.

Chinese irredentism, aggressive behaviour and wilful subversion of established international norms, is what encourages India to establish a deeper and more meaningful relationship with Japan. The two countries, as democracies, understand complications arising out of the emergence of a China that appears to be wanting to rearrange existing institutional and multilateral arrangements in the region with a *Pax Sinica*, where power is not distributed but is a centrifugal force radiating outwards. China's almost unstoppable rise as the primary vector is in economic and strategic terms with an outlook that encourages an Asia, where a plethora of political systems exist under the 'benevolent' tutelage of a China at the centre again after a century of 'humiliation' beginning with the reverses and eventual demise of the Qing dynasty since the Opium Wars of the 1840s.

Beijing's selective use of history has been conflated with the legitimacy of the Communist Party of China (CPC). The selective use of history by Beijing justifies the vilification of neighbours and squelches any independent attempt to intellectually revisit excesses inspired by ideological excesses at home especially during the Great Leap Forward in the late 1950s and the Cultural Revolution from 1966 to 1976.

Will countries like Japan and India be quiescent and accept a Beijing led re-ordering of the Asian geopolitical map or will they align their respective national positions to form a bulwark against this new emerging 'hegemon'? Clearly, the two countries are beginning a long journey to identify common issues that bring them together and China's rise in strategic terms to become the sole arbiter in the Asia-Pacific region motivates New Delhi and Tokyo to increasingly coordinate their shared sense of values and outlook for the region.

(b) Economic

Despite a recent slowdown in India's economy owing to domestic decisions made in the economic sphere especially demonetisation of its currency and introduction of a nation-wide general sales tax doing away with earlier state level taxation regimes, for any investor the sheer appeal of India's large and growing market is an opportunity waiting to be tapped. Japan has been an early investor in India's growth potential and the Overseas Development Assistance (ODA) Tokyo provides to India is the highest it does for any country. It was Japanese ODA that conceptualised and realised the New Delhi metro network–one of the world's largest. Along the lines of the Taiheiyo belt (also known as the Tokaido corridor) extending from Ibaraki prefecture in northern Japan to Fukuoka prefecture in southern Japan, the ODA is providing funding for the Western Dedicated Corridor and the Delhi-Mumbai Industrial Corridor (DMIC) which envisages the setting up of eight new planned industrial townships. The financial outlay for these projects is upwards of USD 90 billion. An industrial corridor between Chennai and Bangalore is also envisaged linking India's automobile hub with the software hub by the generous assistance provided by the ODA on terms extremely favourable. What New Delhi recognises is that ODA funding is not going to constrict economic growth owing to expensive repayment tenures, unlike that faced by Sri Lanka and Pakistan when it comes to Chinese investment in their domestic economy.

Despite the optimism on both sides, the irony of the Japan-India bilateral remains that economic relations between Japan and India are still lagging behind political relations. The bilateral trade between the two countries is to be seen as a prelude, taking into account the actual potential, and institutional arrangements to facilitate trade falling short of the expectations dominating headlines. The Comprehensive Economic Partnership Agreement (CEPA) signed by both the sides has not really taken off with bilateral trade dropping in the past few years. From a high of USD 18.5 billion in 2012-2013, bilateral trade in 2016-2017 was USD 13.5 billion with India's trade deficit being USD 5.9 billion. Japan's high quality and service standards and non-tariff barriers inhibit Indian exporters from making inroads into the Japanese market.

Japan's interest in India stems from the economic opportunities the latter presents to the former. Since the early 1990s, Japan's economic growth has plummeted and the economy growing at a level considered one of the lowest in the OECD. Economic stasis is one side of the story since Japan is a crucible for high technology and world beating firms that are models to be emulated by others. Domestic economic stasis apart, Japan has the financial resources and reserves to invest in a country like India, especially infrastructure. The investible surplus Japan has at its disposal for international investments provides a rate of return that more than balances the negative rate of interest at home. The availability of capital at extremely soft terms from Japan ensures that India will not regress in financial terms while repaying loans unlike other South Asian countries like Sri Lanka and Pakistan who after availing themselves of Chinese loans for cconomic infrastructure are sinking deeper and deeper into an economic morass. Financial servitude to Beijing for the indeterminate future is perhaps the modern version of fealty to the 'middle kingdom'! Murmurs about Beijing's financial hold on Sri Lanka and Pakistan have encouraged a few to opine that the sovereignty these countries hold dear has been bartered away financially and hence strategically.

(c) Political

Japanese prime minister Shinzo Abe's recent election victory reinforces domestic political trends globally where conservative political parties are increasingly dominating the political centre stage in established democracies. Regarding Japan–India relations both the countries have political parties at the helm who represent a conservative outlook in politics domestically and make their propensity to reach out to similar democratic polities an article of faith in their foreign policy behaviour. Modi and Abe represent a conservative outlook in domestic politics and are increasingly putting a personal stamp on bilateral relations by advocating the need for a strategic equivalence.

A common determinant influencing decision-making in Tokyo and New Delhi is China. Beijing's policies in the maritime realm and the mountains bordering India play an important role in the domestic politics of Japan and India to adopt an obdurate stand against China. In New Delhi's case, the humiliating defeat in 1962, to China still reverberates in domestic politics. For Tokyo, the extremely transactional approach to the bilateral adopted by China stumps domestic opinion makers and elected representatives. Until 2003, the ODA Japan provided was weighed heavily in favour of China. Every hostile act by China–verbally and in the maritime domain–against Japan, empowers domestic political expressions that favour a tougher line to be adopted towards Beijing. Matters regarding handling an assertive China get complicated with Washington, long a security umbrella to Japan, is going through its own churning in the domestic political sphere and a coherent foreign policy continuity lacking with the Trump administration forcing Tokyo to look for partners willing to assuage Tokyo's current conundrums regarding Beijing.

If New Delhi and Tokyo have their fair share of domestic actors directing their respective domestic audiences towards the shenanigans from Beijing, it translates into political gains for whichever party is in power by adopting a 'tough and principled' line against Beijing. An important aspect of Tokyo and New Delhi getting closer is the existential challenge posed by a China that is irredentist, aggressive, and displaying intent to use force to effect outcomes suiting its needs. The existing compact of a norm adhering tendency appears to be unravelling with Beijing deciding how to re-order the structures that it feels for long have kept its aspirations shackled.

Analysis

What indeed, is the typology of Japan-India relations?

As Arpita Mathur has cogently argued "(T)he central research question is to decipher whether the relationship that has started building up after a period of benign neglect is just a balancing act in response to the stimulus of China's ascendance in the region or whether there is enough substance and rationale behind it to sustain ties in the future."[3]

For India, the rise of China is poignant, as it was India, whose emergence as a benign new power in Asia's geopolitics was derailed by the war in 1962 with China where India ended up humiliated. It is this humiliation that informs, dominates and unites India's decision-making sections when it comes to Beijing. Added to New Delhi's discomfiture is China's success in transforming its economy and emerging as the world's second largest economy in a relatively short period of around three and a half decades since the Open Door Policy was introduced in 1979 by Deng Xiaoping. Adding to New Delhi's discomfiture is that this economic success has been performed by a state calling itself a 'socialist market economy.'

For Japan, billions of dollars of investments in China, technology transfers, leading corporate decisions involving the setting up of manufacturing units in China, thousands of exchange scholarships for Chinese students to Japanese educational institutions all encouraging China to socialise to a world where norms and institutions moderate most aspects of human activity, have not translated into a gratitude of sorts for Tokyo's faith in investing in a country that is ostensibly socialist but for all practical purposes a market economy. Rather, Japan's investments have been turned and twisted around into a political issue with sporadic violence directed at Japanese investments and factories, while at the political level, manufactured hostility keeps alive excesses committed by Japanese troops in China against the Chinese people. It pays for Beijing to keep alive historical issues that in many ways moulded the ruling CPC into what it is today.

In Japan's case, the ever looming prospect of a powerful China– economically and in strategic terms poses fundamental questions accompanying tepid economic growth for close to three decades and an ageing population making economic growth of the post-world war phase a nostalgic footnote. For India, the tensions of being witness to the rise of China and being isolated in South Asia encourages official 'Act East' policy to have Japan as an economic entrepreneur in India and a strategic partner that dovetails the 'Indo-Pacific' *weltanschauung,* so beloved of strategic analysts in New Delhi visualising for India a central role in the 'Indo-Pacific' scheme of things.

Stretching the argument made earlier, I submit that, strategic symmetry between India and Japan is scripted largely by a common 'uniting' factor in the aggressive and irredentist stance adopted by China to create a future Asia where one centrifugal force radiates power with surrounding countries quiescent and accepting a *Pax Sinica.* In other words, a twenty-first century version of a tributary system where the CPC led China, enforces its writ on Asia where a plethora of political systems exist under the benevolent tutelage of a CPC led China, at the centre and behaving very much like the dynasties of yore and presiding over Asia.

Tokyo and New Delhi can achieve a self-sustaining and mutually enriching relationship if diplomatic initiatives are more than equally matched with tangible cooperation in science and technology, health, cooperation in creating newer technologies that are environment friendly and carbon neutral. Japan's expertise in packaged foods, mass rapid transportation systems, logistics and precision engineering will find an India genuinely welcoming. Social connectivity through increased scholarships for students especially in cutting edge fields like Artificial Intelligence, Robotics, Space, Stealth materials, genetic engineering, Aeronautics, ship building, railway engineering, nuclear power generation with safeguards etc. are specific areas where the two countries can collaborate and create new vistas.

Moving beyond the complementary, it is worth wondering why the Indian Institutes of Technologies (IITs), considered to be crucibles of young aspiring technology professionals in India, have never had any mentoring from Japan. The early IITs were mentored by the US, UK, Germany and the erstwhile Soviet Union…surprisingly not Japan. It is these cobwebs that need to be cleared and Japan welcomed for being just that–Japan–a society where technology has adapted to a civilisation welcoming constant change and not imposing its political or cultural tenets on others. Science and Technology ought to be the new connectivity that overarches strategic calculations and proves to be of endearing strength to the bilateral.

To most people from India, Japan is the central locale of technology and efficiency. There is also a Japan welcoming to tourists. The depreciation in the yen has acted as an incentive for many tourists to consider Japan a tourist destination. However, people to people initiatives between Japan and India should not end up in an institutional *cul de sac* where bureaucratic dominance stifles and not facilitates. Culture also has an important role in leavening the bilateral relationship with Japan's ancient forms like Kabuki finding an equivalent in Kathakali and Yakshagana in India.[4]

Political connectivity through annual summits, a wide ranging and performing Strategic Economic Dialogue between the two sides that implements agreements and bring to fruition many of the recommendations made, economic connectivity through increased investments, structured dispute redressal mechanisms, and enhancing people to people connect are the way ahead for Tokyo and New Delhi.

Japan's diplomatic endeavours are value oriented towards democracies and rather transactional with non-democracies with strong shades of economic necessity motivating the latter, while norm adherence and human values act as powerful determinants with the former. Tokyo-New Delhi relations for long were hostage to the vicissitudes of the Cold War and New Delhi's predilection for a policy of non-alignment constricted India's foreign policy bandwidth. That said, the coalescing of Japan and India should not be determined by China and its belligerence. Rather, it should be a genuine value and norm driven bilateral, not predicated by the existential challenges posed by China to either. A genuine bilateral ought to be guided by strong institutional links–government and societal.

The biggest hurdle to closer Japan–India relations are the respective institutional actors in both the countries. The bureaucracies in Tokyo and New Delhi are known for their stonewalling and intransigence putting paid to hopes raised by political leaderships on both sides heralding a new dawn in bilateral relations. An opening, revealing a bureaucratic thaw in Japan *vis-à-vis* India, was the 'India-Japan Agreement for Cooperation in the Peaceful Uses of Nuclear Energy' signed in November 2016.[5] For a conservative bureaucracy like Japan's, to sign an agreement with a non-NPT member like India on nuclear issues was a revelation, taking into account the genuine domestic abhorring of nuclear weapons and the criticism India faced in 1998 after conducting nuclear tests.

This agreement comes at a time when the security conundrums of Northeast Asia are undergoing change and indicates that institutionally a change in Japan's opinion regarding India has taken place. In return, the Indian bureaucracy, notorious for many reasons, and rated as one of the worst performing in Asia, has to be accommodative of Japan's investment and strategic decisions with India as being articles of faith and not invent or put in place obstacles that would erode faith and divert investment and scientific capital elsewhere, leaving India with the potential to deliver but not in actual, owing to self-imposed constraints. Talented as they are, India's bureaucracy constantly reinvents itself to obstruct initiatives and adopts a Standard Operating Procedure (SOP) of delay and dither citing obtuse rules. The political leaderships in both the countries need to impress upon their bureaucratic servitors to look beyond term limits of the political leaderships that have put in place agreements facilitating the bilateral. Institutional obstruction and stonewalling will only end up hurting India more. Japan's conservative bureaucracy is the mirror image of India's with initiatives taken by the political leadership being stymied by institutional lethargy and even worse an attitude that administratively dilutes any decision since the political leadership in a democracy is bound to respect electoral choices made, while institutional actors are insulated from popular choices and are sequestered largely from public scrutiny.

An aspect that needs mentioning is the stamp of personalities on the bilateral. Shinzo Abe and Narendra Modi are charismatic leaders in their own right and preside over a political spectrum in both the countries where the opposition is fractured and not capable, as of now, of posing a challenge to either. Should either of them be relegated to the opposition or a political sabbatical, will subsequent leaders in both the countries deepen the engagement or allow a drift to take over nullifying the euphoria of the present?

There is no altruism in international politics. It could be construed that Japan is looking beyond the Yoshida doctrine[6] where Japan's security is anchored to the US. Cold War allegiances, where Japan was an intrinsic partner to the US is giving way to a new Cold Peace rearrangement taking place with erstwhile allies in the Cold War cultivating 'fence sitters' like India with its erstwhile NAM credentials to begin to coalesce around a new as yet amorphous grouping united in their suspicions and misgivings of an ever growing China which situates itself as an irredentist power impatient to create a new order with the imprimatur 'Pax Sinica.'

Also, is Japan actively cultivating India to make up for a shortfall from Washington where an extremely virulent domestic agenda appears to have derailed foreign policy owing to an absence of ideas that earlier made United States the gravitational centre of international politics? Pronouncements made by President Donald Trump during his election campaign did not endear himself to Japan, although the practicalities of diplomacy appear to have moderated his tone and tenor when it comes to Tokyo-Washington relations. Or, is the ever growing international presence of China proving to be an existential threat and Japan is finding leadership from the United States waning and the need of the day is to hedge by cultivating Beijing's nemesis, New Delhi?

The answers to questions raised will be clear in a decade or so. Until then *que sera sera....*

Notes

1. 'Japan-India Relations,' Ministry of Foreign Affairs of Japan, 19 January 2017. Available at:http://www.mofa.go.jp/region/asia-paci/india/archives.html (Retrieved on 6 November 2017)
2. "Joint Statement on the Advancement of the Strategic and Global Partnership between Japan and India," Ministry of Foreign Affairs of Japan, October 22, 2008. Available at http://www.mofa.go.jp (Retrieved on 8 November 2017).
3. Arpita Mathur, India-Japan Relations: Drivers, Trends and Prospects, RSIS Monograph, No.23, 2012, p.1.
4. The week-long visit by Emperor Akihito and Empress Michiko to India from 30 November–6 December 2013 has in many ways played a role in influencing and deepening current bonhomie and its consequent spillovers.
5. See 'Agreement between the Government of Japan and the Government of the Republic of India, for Cooperation in the Peaceful uses of Nuclear Energy' signed 11 November 2016. Available at:http://www.mofa.go.jp/files/000202920.pdf (Retrieved on 8 November 2017)
6. Shigeru Yoshida, Japan's first prime minister after the Second World War is considered to be the inspiration behind the founding totem of Japan's post world war policy of focusing on economic reconstruction domestically while its security would be guaranteed by the United States.

Chapter - 6

India-Japan Relations and the Mutuality of Interest in Maritime Security

—Akhter Hussain Khan

Introduction

The friendship between India and Japan has a long history, rooted in spiritual affinity and strong cultural and civilisational ties. The modern nation states have carried on the positive legacy of the old association which has been strengthened by shared values of belief in democracy, individual freedom and the rule of law. Over the years, the two countries have built upon these values and created a partnership based on both principle and pragmatism. Today, India is the largest democracy in Asia and Japan the most prosperous.

India-Japan relations have traditionally and historically been cordial. For centuries, the people of both the countries have had strong cultural ties with each other. These ties were especially strong because of Buddhism which spread from India to Japan, via China and Korea. The cultural exchange between India and Japan is said to have started seemingly around sixth century A.D., with the introduction of Buddhism to Japan. The strong ties between India and Japan are also linked with India's struggle for independence. In this struggle the help provided by Japanese to Netaji Subhash Chandra Bose and Indian National Army (INA) was instrumental which continues to shape the popular perception about Japan among Indian citizens. After World War Second, India and Japan signed a peace treaty in 1949 and also established diplomatic relations on 28th April, 1952.[1]

Despite an overall positive historical legacy, India and Japan could not develop good bilateral relations till the mid 1990s. This low in relations can be attributed to the absence of political will to engage, due to cold war politics both the states were on different tracks. Japan was aligned with the US and India followed a non-alignment strategy in order to keep away from getting entangled into bipolar rivalry.[2] The Indian scholar, Sumit Ganguly aptly points out that India professed a non-aligned foreign policy so as assert its right to pursue its own interests free from any external domination.[3] Leaving aside the India's Non-alignment strategy, officially it was perceived that India is closer to Soviet Union than the US. Thus the atmosphere of cold-war and other geopolitical imperatives led to the divergence in foreign policy objectives between India and Japan. Japan perceived India as a Pro-Soviet state and India saw Japan as a state which toed American line on regional and global issues and thus lacked its own independent political and diplomatic outlook. So, the India-Japan bilateral relations were considered as a story of missed opportunities due to strategic compulsions of Cold War.

After the end of Cold War, the political and the strategic divide between the two countries started waning. The collapse of Soviet Union and the end of Cold War led to some serious rethinking in India's policy circles with special focus on India's foreign policy and foreign economic priorities.[4] In post 1990s era in general and twenty-first century in particular the strategic atmosphere in Asia changed drastically leading to new alignments and balancing as per realist behaviour. The changed atmosphere led to the change in Japan's perception about India and now India is viewed as a significant partner in Asia by Japan.[5] This alteration in outlook is also backed by certain compulsions of protecting national interest in wake of growing assertiveness shown by the neighbouring revisionist power. Also the changing attitude of India and Japan towards each other can be witnessed from many high level visits being exchanged in recent years.

Recent Developments in Relationship Towards Maturity

The growing status of India at both regional and international level was felt by Japan quite recently. The changing perception of Japan about India was evident since August 2000. The Prime Minister of Japan Mori Yoshiro's visit to India was a turning point in India-Japan relations. By declaring that Japan and India are global partners, PM Mori prepared the ground for considering India as an important ally. Subsequently, the December 2006 joint statement focussed on transforming the bilateral relationship into a strategic partnership, and an August 2007 joint statement sought to provide a roadmap for building enduring strategic relationships.[6]

The current Prime Minister of Japan, Shinzo Abe, during his August 2007 visit to India likened his visit to the sentimental visit of his grandfather and Prime Minister of Japan, Nobusuke Kishi, who visited India in 1957 and was received warmly by his counterpart, Jawaharlal Nehru. In reciprocity, Prime Minister Manmohan Singh was invited to Tokyo where he gave a speech at Japanese Diet. In this speech Manmohan Singh sought a strong push for economic ties between the respective countries. He said, "Our trade and investment ties are well below the potential and this must change." Talking about nuclear energy PM Singh said that India considered nuclear power as a viable and clean source of energy and sought Japan's help in putting in place innovative and forward looking approaches of international community to make this possible. Both the Prime Minister's declared 2007 as the India-Japan Friendship year.[7] Subsequently, PM Manmohan Singh visited Japan in 2008 and 2010. During 2008 visit, the two Prime Ministers in the India-Japan Annual Summit reiterated the importance of the Strategic and Global Partnership established in 2006 for the purpose of advancing bilateral cooperation as well as cooperation in regional and multilateral areas with the objective of promoting peace, stability and prosperity in Asia and the world and for harnessing the full potential of India-Japan relations.[8]

In 2010 visit of PM Manmohan Singh, India and Japan signed a comprehensive economic partnership agreement (CEPA). The CEPA, which became effective from August 2011, envisages abolition of tariffs over 94 per cent of the items traded between India and Japan over a period of 10 years. This step is likely to boost trade and investment ties[9]. On 14th September 2017, PM Shinzo Abe paid an official visit to India. The two Prime Ministers held discussions on a wide range of issues under Strategic and Global Partnership between

India and Japan. The two Prime Ministers welcomed significant deepening of bilateral relations in the past three years and growing convergence in the political, economic and strategic interests. They affirmed strong commitment to their values-based partnership in achieving a free, open and prosperous Indo-Pacific Region where sovereignty and international law are respected, and differences are resolved through dialogue. The two Prime Ministers emphasised that India and Japan could play a central role in strengthening the rules-based order. They pledged to work towards:

1. Aligning Japan's Free and Open Indo-Pacific Strategy with India's Act East Policy, including through enhancing maritime security cooperation, improving connectivity in the wider Indo-Pacific region and strengthening ties with ASEAN.
2. Reinforcing their efforts to ensure partnerships for prosperity through the India-Japan Investment Promotion Partnership, speedy implementation of key infrastructure projects including the Mumbai-Ahmedabad High Speed Railway (MAHSR), and advancing cooperation in the fields of energy, smart cities, information and communication technology, space, science and technology, bio-technology, pharmaceuticals and health.
3. Strengthening people-to-people and cultural ties through enhanced Japanese language teaching in India and collaboration in the fields of tourism, civil aviation, higher education, women's education, skills development and sports.
4. On global challenges such as proliferation of Weapons of Mass Destruction (WMDs), terrorism, space and cyber security, United Nations Security Council (UNSC) reform, climate change and environment.
5. Strengthening trilateral cooperation frameworks with the United States, Australia and other countries.[10]

In November 2017, ahead of the East Asia Summit, in Manila, representatives of four democracies (India, Japan, US and Australia) met for consultation on the issue of common interest in the Indo-Pacific region. This meet apparently signalled the renewal of Quad. The renewal of this dormant grouping and the repeated use of the

term Indo-Pacific by US President Donald Trump generated a degree of animation in the strategic circles.[11]

Maritime Security and the Converging Interests

India-Japan relations are multi-faceted. Besides, the focus on economic issues, their relations also encompasses regional security issues, maritime security issues, energy security and United Nations reforms. Thus, the relations which were previously political in nature have attained the strategic status.[12] In the fields of security, as Subhash Kapilla analyses, the operative principle should be that spheres of initiatives and cooperation are restricted to the bilateral context of India-Japan relations. The aim of India-Japan strategic cooperation should not be viewed as a policy of containing China but moderating and engaging proactively China's approaches to Asian and East Asian Security to the extent possible under 'congagement'. Kapilla further observes that:

> without getting overtly drawn into a United States-China strategic confrontation, countries such as Japan and India will be well advised to operate in close cooperation and in sync with each other and which could hopefully provide necessary counter-ballast for ensuring peace and stability in the Asia-Pacific. With Japan and India opting for strategic cooperation, the third big Asian power i.e. China would consequently accord much needed strategic space to these two powers thereby paving the way for a balanced Asian security.[13]

In recent times maritime security has become a concern for all policy-makers and think-tanks. It is because the littoral countries are now faced with multiple challenges like arms trafficking, narco terrorism, illegal migration etc. The increased attacks by pirates on the ships carrying petroleum and other vital resources have not gone down in numbers in spite of talks of international cooperation amongst several countries. These issues highlight the much needed focus to be given on the regional cooperation among more and more states, as they are involved in different economic activities for survival and increased economic prosperity through sea lines of communication (SLOCs). The growing international trade via sea due to globalisation in the post cold war era has brought in the issue of maritime security and now it has come to the centre stage of discussion in the strategic circles. In this way Indian ocean and some of the straits in it like straits of Hormuz, Straits of Malacca, Lombok and the Sunda straits have acquired great importance as far as the global trade is concerned.[14] Given the fear of international terrorism, the Indian Ocean Sea Lanes remain vulnerable, especially due to the presence of hostile terror outfits in Pakistan and Afghanistan. Thus, any disruption in the sea traffic can spoil the growing economic prospectus of the countries in the region and others at large. Majority of the energy supplies to littoral states are now through sea routes and any disruption in their flow can have disastrous consequences. Moreover, scarce energy resources have now become a critical factor in geopolitical strategies of many countries and thus any disruption can result in serious security problems. Littoral countries, therefore, need to be sensitive about the security of the SLOCs. India, which is more energy dependent for its economic growth needs to secure SLOCs. Moreover, due to China's rise in the Indian Ocean Region, which is also energy hungry, India needs to look seawards.[15]

The China's presence in Asia has many security implications for both Japan and India. China is also projecting its naval power in the region. For example, China's naval ambitions in the East China Sea region have caused uneasiness in Tokyo. In November 2004, a Chinese nuclear submarine penetrated into Japan's water near Okinawa. Moreover, some other problems which add to this political divide are, the territorial dispute over the Senkaku/Diaoyu Islands[16], problems of rights over gas fields in the East China Sea; Japan's close relations with Taiwan; China's memories of atrocities created by Japan during pre-Second World War period etc.[17] Also, in the Indian Ocean it is clear from the China's 'string of pearls'[18] policy that China wants to protect the SLOCs in the Indian ocean and restrain India's naval outreach. This policy also is a clear indication of China's intentions to have dominant influence in the Indian Ocean region.[19]

Japan essentially being a maritime nation depends on the oceans for its resources and external trade. Almost 90 per cent of Japan's oil needs come from the Persian Gulf region. This means that any hindrance in the normal movement of oil supplies can have serious repercussions on Japan's economy. Similarly, various economic and strategic interests of India are dependent on security of Indian Ocean. Though India had a long maritime history, it was more focussed landwards due to various border issues with China and Pakistan and paid less attention seawards. The geographic location of India gives it the strategic advantage in the Indian Ocean and thus can play an important role in maintaining rule-based order at sea. India is sandwiched between the two most important choke points for global oil supplies (the Straits of Mallaca to its East and Straits of Hormuz to its west). After the end of Cold War, New Delhi has pursued a comprehensive maritime strategy which entails development of ports and harbours, exploitation of marine resources and expansion of commercial shipping.[20]

Being democracies, both India and Japan have supported freedom of navigation and over flight, civil aviation safety, unimpeded lawful commerce, and peaceful settlement of disputes in accordance with international law. Where there is convergence of interests, India has always invested in strengthening relations with the like-minded countries.[21] The shared commitment towards protecting sea lines of communication as a 'public good' for the region also goes in favour of enhanced maritime cooperation between India and Japan and the next step in this direction should be knowing each other's operational concept.[22] Japan has highly depended on the US Navy for safeguarding some SLOCs, but now it has started taking cognizance of India's growing capabilities as far as securing SLOCs is concerned. India, in fact can play a productive role in SLOCs. Besides protecting the energy interests, the straits like Malacca Strait, are exposed to the dangers of piracy and terror incidents. India has extended cooperation during the 1999 M/V Alondra Rainbow piracy incident which subsequently led to confidence-building and a robust framework of cooperation between the coast guards and navies of both the countries.[23]

The Malabar exercises were started by Indian and US Navy in 1992. Japan also participated in many drills from 2007.[24] This participation of Japan in Malabar exercises has irritated China, which forced India to discontinue it. But the early revival of India-US-Japan trilateral exercises proves that there is a more strong maritime policy on the Indian side. The off and on appearance of China's nuclear submarines in Indian Ocean and the construction of Chinese first overseas military base in Djibouti (in the Horn of Africa)[25] are the reasons which extend India-Japan maritime cooperation to the Indian Ocean.

In November 2011, India's Defence Minister A.K. Antony visited Japan and agreed to conduct bilateral naval exercises. To operationalise the agreement, the first Japan-India Maritime bilateral exercise codenamed JIMEX-12 was conducted by Indian Navy with Japanese Maritime Self Defence Force in June 2012.[26] Recently on 14th September 2017, the two Prime Ministers commended the significant progress made in maritime security cooperation evidenced by the expansion in scale and complexity of the MALABAR Exercise in the Bay of Bengal. They noted the ongoing close cooperation between the Indian Navy and Japan Maritime Self-Defence Force (JMSDF) in various specialised areas of mutual interest, including anti-submarine aspects. They also acknowledged the importance of bilateral cooperation in maritime security by strengthening and enhancing exchanges in expanding maritime domain awareness (MDA) in the Indo-Pacific region.[27]

Balancing the China's Rise

The China factor in relations between India and Japan became more important after the April 2005 anti-Japan demonstrations in China. During Koizumi Junichiro's visit to India in April 2005, a major step was taken in the form of an Action Plan called the 'Eight Fold initiative for strengthening India-Japan Global Partnership'. This Action Plan clearly indicated the resolve of the two countries to enhance bilateral security dialogue and cooperation. It was decided to: (1) strengthen service to service exchanges between defence establishments of the two countries, (2) working to ensure the safety and security of Maritime traffic through joint exercises against piracy and annual Japan Coast Guard-Indian Coast Gaurd talks and (3) building up cooperation between the Maritime Self-Defence Force and Indian Navy in recognition of the importance of Maritime Security.[28]

The rising trajectory of China (economically as well as politically) has brought in lot of political and strategic concerns for both India and Japan. China's presence in Asia can have security implications for both India and Japan. Both countries are concerned about growing assertion of China.[29] The instances of docking of submarines by China in Colombo, Gwadar etc is the indicator of ever expanding forays of People's Liberation Army-Navy (PLA-N) in the Indian Ocean Region. Also China's forging of extensive maritime links with eastern Africa, Seychelles, Mauritius, Maldives, Sri Lanka, Bangladesh, Myanmar and Cambodia can be aimed at a "strategic encirclement" of India.[30] Prime Minister Modi during his visit to the smaller Indian Ocean island states in March 2015, had laid out a strategic 'blue-print' for the Indian Ocean that includes an element of continuous maritime engagement with littoral neighbours. It must now be broadened to include an element of structured maritime engagement with key Indo-Pacific states.[31]

Regional security situation has been worsening in recent years in the Indo-Pacific. China's rapid rise has been causing anxieties in New Delhi. Japan has been sparring with China in the East China Sea while India was recently engaged in a long stand-off with China on the Doklam Plateau. The China-Pakistan Economic Corridor (CPEC), which is a part of One Belt One Road (OBOR) initiative of China and other strategies of China for the influence in South Asia, necessitates India to look for allies. Beijing's 'string of pearls' policy consists of setting up of military and naval facilities in the India's immediate neighbourhood like in Myanmar, Pakistan and Bangladesh has raised fears in New Delhi about naval encirclement of India. China's aggressive foreign policy is making it imperative for regional powers to collaborate and cooperate.[32] The South China Sea issue and the stand that China has shown by refusing to accept the Permanent Court of Arbitration's ruling shows how important it is for India and Japan to come together so as to protect their strategic national interest. The increasing tension on the Korean Peninsula and the security threat emerging from the recent nuclear tests by North Korea has prompted Japan to look for allies in order to balance the changing security architecture in Asia. This gives India an opportunity to play a role befitting its rising status and subsequently pursue its national interest.

Conclusion

The bilateral relations between India and Japan is witnessing the best period in history. PM Abe's words that "The India-Japan relationship has the greatest potential of any bilateral relationship in the world" are reflective of this productive period in the relationship.[33] This is an indication of growing importance of India in foreign policy calculus of Japan. Though both being successful democracies, their like-mindedness in other ways also makes their relationship stronger. This rapid deepening of ties after the end of Cold War in general and since the onset of twenty-first century has been based on growing recognition of convergences in the political, economic, security and strategic fields. Relations have transformed and reached to the level of Special Strategic and Global Partnership. There is an emerging consensus on contemporary issues of peace, security and development; and new common regional and global challenges, where much can be achieved by working together. This has been manifest in cooperation in the area of maritime security like participation of Japan in Malabar Naval exercises.[1]

References

1. Reetika Sharma, Ramvir Goria, Vivek Mishra, *India and the Dynamics of World Politics : A book on Indian Foreign Policy, Related events and International Organisations.*(New Delhi: Pearson Publishers, 2011) p. 1.254. Also see Ministry of Foreign Affairs, India-Japan Relations. http://www.mofa.go.jp/region/asia-paci/india/data.html
2. Madhuchanda Ghosh, "India and Japan's Growing Synergy: From a Political to a Strategic Focus." *Asian Survey* 48, no. 2 (2008): 284.
3. Sumit Ganguly, "India's foreign policy grows up." *World Policy Journal* 20, no. 4 (2004): 41-47.
4. Rajaram Panda, "Introduction", in *India and Japan: Multi-Dimensional Perspectives*, ed. Rajaram Panda and Kazuo Ando. (New Delhi: Japan Foundation, 1997), 1.
5. Madhuchanda Ghosh, "India and Japan's Growing Synergy: From a Political to a Strategic Focus." p. 285.
6. *Ibid.*, p. 283.
7. K. Venugopal, "Manmohan for big push to ties with Japan", *The Hindu*, March 22, 2012.

8. Ministry of External Affairs, Government of India, "Joint Statement on the Advancement of the Strategic and Global Partnership between India and Japan" October 22, 2008. http://www.mea.gov.in/bilateral-documents.htm?dtl/5395/Joint_Statement_on_the_Advancement_ of_the_Strategic_and_Global_Partnership_between_India_and_Japan. See also the Minstry of Foreign Affairs of Japan, http://www.mofa.go.jp/region/asia-paci/india/pmv0810/joint_s.html
9. Vinay Kaura, "India-Japan Relations and Asia's Emerging Geopolitics." *Indian Journal of Asian Affairs* 29, no. 1/2 (2016): 26. http://www.jstor.org/stable/44123127.)
10. Ministry of External Affairs, Government of India, "India-Japan Joint Statement during visit of Prime Minister of Japan to India", September 1, 2017. http://www.mea.gov.in/bilateral-documents.htm?dtl/28946/IndiaJapan_Joint_Statement_during_visit_of_Prime_Minister_of_Japan_to_India_September_14_2017.
11. Arun Prakash, "The wind in India's sails", *Indian Express.* November 24, 2017.
12. Vinay Kaura, "India-Japan Relations and Asia's Emerging Geopolitics." p 17.
13. Cited in, M. B. Alam, "Re-balancing within Asia: An Analytical Study of India-Japan Relations", in *Emerging India in the New World Order,* Ed. M. B. Alam and Nisar-ul-Haq. (New Delhi: Bloomsbury Publishers, 2015) 189-190.
14. Biswajit Mohapatra, "Maritime Security in India's Neighbourhood and Indian Ocean: Challenges and Strategies," *in India and Her Neighbours: Towards a Proactive Partnership*, ed. Mohammad Badrul Alam. (New Delhi: Kalpaz Publications, 2015). 35-36.
15. *Ibid.*
16. Madhuchanda Ghosh, "India and Japan's Growing Synergy: From a Political to a Strategic Focus". p. 284.
17. Lalima Varma, "Enhancing Strategic Ties between Japan and India:Japan-China relations as a factor", in Takenori Horimoto and Lalima Varma (eds), India-Japan Relations in Emerging Asia, p. 41.
18. C. Raja Mohan, "Chinesetakeaway: String of Pearls", *Indian Express,* June 11, 2014.
19. Bill Gertz, "China Builds up Strategic Sea Lanes," *Washington Times*, January 18, 2005.
20. Vinay Kaura, "India-Japan Relations and Asia's Emerging Geopolitics." p. 23.
21. M. B. Alam, "Re-balancing within Asia: An Analytical Study of India-Japan Relations," in Emerging India in the New World Order, Ed. M. B. Alam and Nisar-ul-Haq. (New Delhi: Bloomsbury Publishers, 2015) 190.

22. Marie Izuyama, 'India, Japan and Maritime Security Cooperation in the Asia Pacific', in Takenori Horimoto and Lalima Varma (eds), India-Japan Relations in Emerging Asia, p. 195.
23. Titli Basu, "India-Japan and the 'Confluence of Two Seas': Ten yeas on", *IDSA Issue Brief.* 3-4.
24. "Malabar naval exercise: All you need to know in 10 points", *The Times of India,* July 10, 2017.
25. "China sends troops to Djibouti for opening of military base", *The Indian Express,* July 12, 2017.
26. Vinay Kaura, "India-Japan Relations and Asia's Emerging Geopolitics." p. 23.
27. Ministry of External Affairs, Government of India, "India-Japan Joint Statement during visit of Prime Minister of Japan to India", September 1, 2017. http://www.mea.gov.in/bilateral-documents.htm?dtl/28946/IndiaJapan_Joint_Statement_during_visit_of_Prime_Minister_of_Japan_to_India_September_14_2017.
28. Lalima Varma, "Enhancing Strategic Ties between Japan and India:Japan-China relations as a factor", p. 52.
29. Madhuchanda Ghosh, "India and Japan's Growing Synergy: From a Political to a Strategic Focus". p. 292.
30. Rajit Pandit, "India suspicious as Chinese submarine docks in Sri Lanka", *Times of India,* September 28, 2014. https://timesofindia.indiatimes.com/india/India-suspicious-as-Chinese-submarine-docks-in-Sri-Lanka/articleshow/43672064.cms
31. Abhijit Singh, "Deciphering China's Submarine Deployments in the Indian Ocean Region" July 8, 2015. https://idsa.in/idsacomments/Deciphering ChinasSubmarine Deployment sintheIndianOceanRegion_asingh_080715
32. Harsh V. Pant, "China's belligerence has cemented India-Japan relationship" Observers Research Foundation, September 15, 2017. http://www.orfonline.org/research/chinas-belligerence-has-cemented-india-japan-relationship/
33 "India-Japan bilateral relationship has greatest potential: Abe" *The Hindu,* Nov 21, 2015.

threat of international terrorism to them and looks at the plausible options available to the two to pool their efforts to take on the menace.

Trajectory of Relations

Despite having, historically, a rich and chequered cultural ties, the most significant manifestation of which may arguably be the spread of Buddhism in Japan, the two countries could not raise the level of their ties in the post second-world war times to that of strategic one, obviously due to geographical as well as, in many respects, psychological distance between the two.[1] Though after independence, India factored Japan in her interactions with the rest of the world, the inception of ties between the two countries appeared to be more symbolic than substantive in nature. With little commonality of interests in sight apparently owing to the cold war dynamics, it took ten years for the two countries to organise the highest level official visit of their respective leaders. In 1957, the Japanese Prime Minister Nobusuke Kishi came to India and his visit was reciprocated by Pandit Nehru in the same year. Though concrete outcomes of these visits were not significant, two points stand out clearly. Firstly, the exchange of highest level of official visits bore testimony to the prevailing sense of goodwill between the two countries which could have been capitalised on any future opportune time. Secondly, economic ties were identified to be the core concern of the two to build up their relations in the years to come. The limited outcome of the first Prime Minister level visits between the two countries may probably be explained by the seemingly incompatible positions taken by the two countries during the cold war times. Given Japan's close proximity to the United States (US) which in some way also put fetters on the functional autonomy of the former in international affairs, India could not have entered into a close all round relationship, including strategic one, with Japan at a time when she i.e. India was trying to give shape to the non-aligned movement along with other developing countries. The first phase of the Indo-Japan ties was therefore in the nature of an exploratory exercise out of which the two could identify the cultural and economic ties to be the benchmarks of their mutual relationship.

The next phase of the Indo-Japan ties may be taken to have begun in 1961 with the visit of the Japanese Prime Minister Hayato Ikeda to

Chapter - 7

Indo-Japan Strategic Ties: The Perspective of International Terrorism

—Rajendra Kumar Pandey

Though Indo-Japan ties range to almost all the probable dimensions of the cordial relations between two friendly countries, their strategic dimensions appear to be a novel idea taking place in the wake of new political role that Japan took upon itself in the post-cold war times. In view of the complex geo-political circumstances prevailing in the South-East Asia, both the countries found it pertinent to forge a strategic tie between the two. Though the Indo-Japan strategic ties aim at ensuring the persistence of peaceful co-existence amongst all the countries of the region, an unconventional aspect of this tie happens to be the advent of the menace of international terrorism in the aftermath of the 9/11 which is spreading its tentacles to all parts of the world, without any concession to either India or Japan. While India's experiences with the phenomenon of international terrorism is quite comprehensive and goes back to the days of her gaining independence, Japan has also not been immune to this phenomenon. However, the threat of international terrorism to Japan becomes really serious for at least two reasons in contemporary times. Firstly, being an ally of the US, the Japanese would always remain an enemy of those who despise the former. Secondly, the geo-political circumstances are such in the South-East Asia that Japan would turn out to be at the receiving end of the terrorist groups, seeking a foothold in the region. The paper, thus, seeks to analyse the nature of strategic partnership between the two countries, with special reference to the

India. Coming to India with the high expectations of receiving a good response to his efforts in wooing India for closer economic ties, Mr Ikeda was in for a big disappointment as India failed to reciprocate his efforts ostensibly due to the adoption of a socialistic economic policy by then, which would not have been found in consonance with the capitalist economic system prevailing in Japan.[2] Thus, the newly found ground of economic cooperation for taking their mutual relations to greater heights could not be sustained for obvious reasons and the two countries remained without any focus in their dormant relationship. Though Mrs. Indira Gandhi visited Japan in 1969, albeit without much achievements, the decades of sixties, seventies and half of eighties remained mainly, if not totally, uneventful in so far as the relationship between India and Japan is concerned. In the absence of any innovative thinking on part of the political leadership of the two countries with regard to their relationship, coupled with the dynamics of the cold war, in which the two countries found themselves placed on the wrong sides of the game, the bilateral relations between the two countries remained static at the level of an abject pessimism towards each other with no loss and no profit seemingly involved in the dealings.

The stagnation in the Indo-Japan ties was broken in 1984 with the visit of the Japanese Prime Minister Mr.Y Nakasone to India with a vision and commitment to put the Indo-Japan ties on a higher pedestal, heralding the third phase of the Indo-Japan ties. A person with a futuristic and strategic vision, Mr. Nakasone recognised the strategic importance of India in the region and set on to revitalise Japan's relations with India. Matching the initiative of Mr. Nakasone, Indian Prime Minister Rajiv Gandhi also attached great importance to India's relations with Japan and visited Japan thrice during his tenure as the Prime Minister. Given the re-intensification of the cold war during the decade of 1980s, this renewed vigour in the Indo-Japan ties was something which could be attributed only to the mature statesmanship and visionary strategic perspective of the political leadership in the two countries. While the roots of the transformed outlook of Japan towards India might probably lie in the apparent discontinuation of Japanese perspective of looking at India more or less as a local power, always hyphened with Pakistan, the Indian vision was presumably sharpened by the emergence of Japan as the economic giant of Asia and an urge in the Indian leadership to gain from increased interaction with that country.

The upwardly mobile Indo-Japan ties remained on track during much of the decade of 1990s also till the Indian nuclear tests in 1998 ruptured the process with Japan taking a strong stand against these tests on the plea of its non-proliferation policies. However, this temporary setback to their ties was fortunately not allowed to eclipse the brighter prospects for the two countries to evolve a global partnership in the wake of the rapid transformations taking place in the global politics. Hence, realising the futility of continuing with the sour relations between the two countries, Japanese Prime Minister Mr. Y Mori visited India in 2000 and Indian Prime Minister Atal Bihari Vajpayee visited Tokyo in 2001 and both sides announced a joint declaration to consolidate the Indo-Japan global partnership.[3]

In the current phase of the Indo-Japan ties, the one step forward-two steps backward relationship between the two countries as prevailing in the twentieth century was put on high velocity in the new millennium with the thoroughly transformed politico-strategic architecture in the Asia-Pacific region[4] on the one hand and the identification of a number of commonalities between the national interests of the two countries in the prevailing circumstances, on the other. Given the periodic menacing moves emanating from North Korea coming as a direct threat to Japan, and the China's rising military capability and its ambivalent intention of use of force to change the status quo in regions such as South China Sea/Taiwan Straight.[5] Japan is definitely in search of strategic partners with the common vision of meeting the challenges arising out of Chinese strategic posturing in the region. India fits the bill in this regard to a large extent.

More significant are, however, the commonalities of interests[6] in a number of sectors like the economic cooperation, common approaches and concerns on a range of regional issues to become the anchors of an arc of stability, key membership of the emerging concert of democracies, cooperation to reinforce the trends towards multipolarity, reforms in the United Nations Security Council etc. For instance, Japanese investment in India constitutes one of the foremost sources of foreign direct investment in the country though "the economic part of the relationship still remains far below potential."[7] Nonetheless, the two countries are trying to further deepen their relations, apart from diversifying them. In this context, the much fulfilling visit of the Japanese Prime Minister Mr. Shinzo Abe to India in 2007 signifies the newer dimensions being added to the traditionally cordial relations between the two countries.[8]

Contemporaneously, Indo-Japan relations are scaling greater heights with the unique chemistry of personal relations between the current Prime Ministers of the two countries. With the emergence of the 'Modi Doctrine', the primary objective of the Indian foreign policy has got redirected from the Look East Polity to that of the Act East Policy in which Japan occupies the pivotal position.[9] The Act East Policy is, in fact, intended to be the main launching pad to propel India to the position of the key economic and strategic partner of the east Asian countries amidst the growing influence of China in the region.[10] In the new matrix of the Indo-Japan relations, while keeping economic ties at the core, the two are also giving concrete shape to a new geostrategic quadrilateral framework in which US and Australia are also becoming pillars of an arrangement aimed at long-term containment of Chinese adventurous maneuvers in the region.[11] At the same time, the two countries are also emphasising counter-terrorism as one of the common security interests. Thus, in the present times, Indo-Japan relations are probably at the all time high in both range and intensity, with even greater expansion being visualised with each passing day.

Strategic Ties

Conceptually, the term strategic stands for those interactive decisions of people or states that allow for conflict and utilise the cooperation, and strategy means a plan of action suitable to materialise such decisions.[12] Another analyst conceptualises 'strategic' in terms of certain common traits like geopolitical and/or ideological convergence, military-security cooperation, political convergence, closer economic relations, and shared strategic interests.[13] Hence when we talk in terms of Indo-Japan strategic ties, our focus is on almost all those aspects of the relation between the two countries which powerfully impinge on their national interest, and it would be beneficial for the two if they join hands together to meet the challenges jointly.[14] This section presents a bird's eye view of the prospective areas of strategic partnership between the two countries having wider implications particularly for security and defence.[15]

First, though terrorism has remained a menace to India for a long period of time, it has attained international dimensions since 11 September 2001, stretching its reach to almost all parts of the world through the networks mainly, if not exclusively, of al-Qaeda and Islamic State (IS). Having their strongholds in what is called as the 'global Balkans'[16] and drawing support from the unstable geo-political situations prevailing in the region, the international terrorism manifested prominently in the continued disturbed conditions in Afghanistan, Syria and Iraq. Indeed, the spectre of international terrorism has been on the prowl to feed on any and all the countries supposed to be the ally of the US in its game plan in these countries. In such a scenario, both India and Japan have been placed in a precarious situation of not only protecting themselves from the probable attacks from the international terrorists but also design a more prominent role in helping to secure the world peace and security in the future by assisting in stabilisation of the conditions in the region. Cooperation between the two countries has, in fact, already been forthcoming on this point, as illustrated by the Japanese Maritime Self-Defence Force (JMSDF) manoeuvres in the Indian Ocean during the offensive against the Taliban in Afghanistan. But as coalition led forces struggle to calm the area, it is argued by experts that there exists a further scope for India and Japan to join hands through the United Nations (UN) and help secure a more stable future for disturbed regions.

Second, a related issue with the phenomenon of international terrorism is the matter of checking the proliferation of the weapons of mass destructions (WMD) into the hands of the terrorist groups or other fundamentalist groups operating in the countries like Pakistan. Moreover, the discovery of trade links between Pakistan and North Korea over sensitive nuclear weapons technology happened to be a shocking reminder that WMD proliferation was a real and persisting threat demanding serious attention from the countries having stakes in its checking. Interestingly, while North Korea has been viewed as the immediate trouble spot for Japan, the revelations of the nexus between the North Korea and Pakistan on the matter of nuclear technology transfer sent shock waves between India and Japan. Though Japan did not take the nuclear explosion by India in 1998 kindly, its primary concern now seems more to be putting the control and command system of the nuclear arsenals in safe hands. In this respect also, India and Japan share a common concern to check the pilferage of WMDs into the hands of the rogue states and terrorist elements.

Third, the imperatives of energy security have propelled India and Japan to seek an enhanced level of strategic partnership between the two countries. As a matter of fact, while Japan is the world's third largest oil importer relying heavily upon the West Asian supplies, the robust economic growth in India catapulted India also into the category of the prime oil importers in the world. In such a situation, learning lessons from the oil crisis of 1970s, the two countries are trying to diversify their sourcing of oil from other regions of the world also. The peace and security in the West Asia remains a top priority for the both countries. The option available for the two countries in this regard, therefore, appears to be two fold. One, with the earnest attempt to bring peace and order in Afghanistan, Syria and Iraq, the move should also be started for ensuring rapid reconstruction and stabilisation of the situations in these countries. At the same time, India and Japan, being close allies of the US, need to exert as much pressure on the US as possible in order to dissuade it from taking any misadventurous steps in the case of Iran while persuading Iran also to desist from indulging into unscrupulous and illegitimate activities on the nuclear front in violations of the International Atomic Energy Agency (IAEA) regulations.

Fourth, India and Japan finds much scope for partnership in maritime and naval spheres owing to a number of common concerns between the two countries.[17] Given the Japanese position as a maritime nation depending overwhelmingly on the seas both for energy transportation as well as fishing resources, anxiety over the freedom of navigation has grown with particular doubts being cast over the safe passage of ships in the East China Sea and Straight of Hormuz.

Moreover, in recent years the rising tide of international terrorism in South and South East Asia with the menace attaining alarming proportions in the seas around Indonesia and the Arabian Sea, as manifested in the Mumbai attacks on 26 November 2008 by the terrorists taking sea routes to reach their destination, the concern for maritime security has started getting greater attention in the Indo-Japan strategic partnership. Consequently, Japan now looks at India as its prime strategic partner in securing the seas from the menace of both the pirates as well as the terrorists. India, being a reliable naval power in the region has been found propitious by Japan to partner with it in the wake of its growing naval involvement in the Arabian Sea for providing logistical support to peace keeping operations in Afghanistan. In fact, any prospective defence cooperation between India and Japan is supposed to be heavily tilted towards cooperation in the naval field. Japan also values the utmost contribution made by the Indian Coast Guard in protecting the cargo ships from the pirates in the seas at times, and thus seeks to strengthen the coast guard to coast guard cooperation also.

Fifth, Indo-Japan strategic ties gain added significance in view of the China factor weighing in the strategic calculations of both the countries. Despite both India and Japan having strong preferences for increasing bilateral trade with China, the security related issues compel both the countries to position themselves in such a way as to counter any threatening move by China effectively.[18] While Japan is primarily concerned about the Chinese policy towards Taiwan and any probable move on the part of China to change the status quo of the Taiwan Straight, India's prime concern remains rooted in its border disputes with its giant neighbour. In such a scenario, both India and Japan find themselves as the natural ally in the face of any move on the part of China which seeks to undermine the strategic position of either of the two. However, the two countries do not want to play up the issue in such a way so as to jeopardize their positive engagements with China. Their pursuits towards China still remain focused on increasing the volume of trade and enhance the scope of other positive interactions and exchanges with China. Nevertheless, the China factor in the safety and security of both the countries remain a permanent factor and the

Indo-Japan strategic ties reflect the existence of this prominent factor in their relations.

In sum, the range of strategic partnership between India and Japan now covers almost all the probable avenues. The regularity with which the top leadership of the two countries are visiting each other, and seeking to forge both bilateral and multilateral partnerships appears to be the pointer of the shape of things to come in future. In this pursuit, the two countries are also trying to readjust their conventional doctrinal focus and foreign policy objectives to accommodate each other's concerns and interests as much as possible. That way, Indo-Japan strategic ties are likely to be one of the greatest achievements of the Indian foreign policy in contemporary times.

International Terrorism

India has been at the receiving end of the international terrorism much before the menace became endemic to other important countries in the world like the United States. Ironically, the stark reminder to the US in the form of the 9/11 that the phenomenon of international terrorism is for real and no country in the world could remain immune from its sinister designs and onslaughts happens to bear the testimony to the Indian argument before the US that all sorts of terrorism are some kind of hidden enemies which can hit even their erstwhile promoters and supporters. In other words, the grim reality which India has been facing for a number of years became a matter of concern for other major countries in the world only when they themselves got the taste of the demon. Now, India has been joined by several other countries to be the prime targets of the network of international terrorism, carried forward by the radical Islamists in the main. Indeed, the situation has become so precarious for almost all the countries that none of them finds themselves in a position to tackle the menace single-handedly, necessitating the formation of a global front against the international terrorism.

Though not facing the menace of international terrorism to the degree faced by India, Japan had neither been nor is immune to the threats of some sort of terrorism. Indeed, it is startling to note that the pro-imperial nationalism that led to the Meiji restoration in Japan in 1868 was accompanied by frequent terrorist attacks on Tokugawa Shogunate.[19] In recent times also, the Japanese experiences in bearing the burnt of terrorist activities are multiple. For instance, the 'Chukaka-Hu' (Middle Core Faction) was active up through the very early 1990s, attacking police stations or targets associated with the imperial family, and sometimes, foreign interests in Japan, especially airports. The smaller and much more deadly terrorist group, the Japanese Red Army attacked in Japan and then increasingly only outside the country, the climax of which reached in 1996 high profile hostage holding in the Lima Embassy of Japan.[20] Another horrible instance of the act of terrorism in Japan happens to be the release of chemical agent Sarin in a Tokyo subway in May 1995 by the followers of the cult of Aum Shinri Kyo.

The menace of international terrorism has become most formidable in the wake of 9/11 for at least two reasons in contrast to the spectre of terrorism existing in the previous times. Firstly, in the past, the terrorist groups had their prime targets as only certain particular countries like Israel or India and there existed no second level of targets for such groups, thereby confining their area of interest to these countries only. However, after 9/11 a perceptible change appears to have taken place in the outlook of the terrorist groups. Now, having identified the US as their prime target, they have also chosen a number of secondary levels of targets in terms of those countries and interests which happen to be associated with the US. Thus, with the direct targeting of the US interests, having taken the sole superpower as their enemy number one, within and outside the country, the terrorist groups have somewhat expanded their sphere of operation to almost all parts of the world, for, the US allies as well as interests are scattered all over the globe, with Japan and India standing prominently on this count.

Secondly, in the previous times, there existed a number of terrorist groups based in different countries and having their distinct area of operation. Such groups functioned in somewhat disorganised and uncoordinated manner presumably given their lack of contact with each other at times and mutual antipathy at others. In such a scenario, the nature of terrorism could not attain international dimensions for obvious reasons. But now with the advent of al-Qaeda and the IS, the menace of terrorism has truly become international owing to the seemingly widespread network of these organisations, in most, if not all, parts of the world. Moreover, the other smaller terrorist groups operating in various countries now look upon them as the coordinating monoliths and are perhaps willing to accept their leadership role in carrying out the terrorist operations in different parts of the world. Thus, the terrorist attack might have taken place in any part of the world or might have been carried out by even local terrorist groups, the imprint of the al-Qaeda or the IS influence in planning and execution of the terrorist attack becomes distinct.

In the transformed milieu of the objectives and operational methodology of the international terrorism, the vulnerability of India and Japan to the international terrorism needs to be explained. Given India's brush with the onslaughts of terrorism for a fairly long time, this menace has only added new dimensions and lethality to the existing phenomenon of terrorism in the country. However, the expansion of the terrorist activities in South Asia would definitely propel India to become an important force to take on the rise of international terrorism in the region.[21] But for Japan, things appear to have taken a serious turn in real sense as a survey on the perceptions of Japanese students on terrorism and other security problems has found terrorism reckoned as the second most pressing concern of the people.[22] Thus, Japan, indeed, had its share of terrorism in the past. But the menace of terrorism in Japan was not formidable enough to pose any long-term and serious threat to the socio-economic or political system of the country. However, the arrival of the international terrorism on the scene in the aftermath of the 9/11 appears to have made the things tougher for Japan for at least three reasons. In this first place, with Japan remaining a close ally of the US and the prised US interests including the US bases in Okinawa, Misawa, Yokosuka and Saseba remaining positioned in Japan, there seems to be a strong likelihood that, sooner or later, Japan is bound to become a prime target of the terrorist groups bent on harming the interests of the US and its allies.

Second, given the increasing involvement of the Japanese Self Defence Forces in the military operations mounted by the US led forces as in Iraq and Afghanistan, Japan is emerging as one of the strong supporters of the US in its operations in the areas from which the terrorist groups draw their sustenance. Moreover, in the aftermath of the 9/11, Japan volunteered itself to be a dependable ally of the US in its war against international terrorism.[23] In such a scenario, there exists a probability that Japan, like Britain might emerge as a primary target of the terrorist groups instead of presently remaining a secondary target of such groups.

Finally, as the terrorist groups may seek a foothold in the South-Eastern Asia countries,[24] Japan being an important country in the region, is bound to be adversely affected. Indeed, the growing menace of the international terrorism in the region has induced US and in turn Japan to take a tough posture against such groups. Consequently, Japan has become one of the frontline states in the region to take on the monster of the international terrorism.

Thus, with both India and Japan facing the spectre of international terrorism in one way or another, there existed ample opportunity for the two to write a new chapter in their strategic relations. Given India's own long standing fight against terrorism and her urge to enter into strategic relations with other countries to evolve a joint front against international terrorism, Japan was definitely well placed to benefit from the experiences of India in this regard. With the turnaround in the security perspective of Japan in the wake of the 9/11, whereby a cardinal principle of its long-term security strategy becomes the 'cooperation with other countries in combating terrorism,'[25] the stage appeared to be set for India and Japan to enter into an agreement to meet the challenges of international terrorism jointly.

Though India and Japan have been issuing joint statements on countering international terrorism in the aftermath of the 9/11, the first step towards concretizing such oral assertions came in the form of the setting up of the Japan-India Joint Working Group on Counter-Terrorism in 2006.[26] The issue was specially highlighted during the visit of Indian Prime Minister Manmohan Singh to Tokyo. The two countries not only agreed for close bilateral cooperation on the issue but also called upon the members of the United Nations to work together for the adoption of a comprehensive convention on elimination of international terrorism, thereby giving a multilateral texture to the fight against the menace. The Indo-Japan cooperation against international terrorism has become sharper and more focused now with the growing gelling of their national interests.

Concluding Observation

The trajectory of Indo-Japan relations are a classic case of complete turnaround in the relations between two countries that began their interaction on a somewhat subdued note. The age old cultural exchanges between the two countries could not prove formidable enough to overcome the constraints of cold war and catapult the cultural ties into a comprehensive framework of strategic relations between the two. While the cold war dynamics set the backstage of lethargic relations between the two countries, lack of vision and personal chemistry between the top political leadership of the two may also be considered as the significant factor inhibiting expansion of the range and depth of strategic relations between them. Thus, the relations between two important countries having close cultural interactions and with enormous potential for extending the range and depth of relations to limitless proportions, remained almost captive to the extraneous forces of cold war politics.

But such a state of relations between the two countries appeared to be unnatural given the existence of multitude of avenues of closest ties between them. So, once the shackles of the cold war were shattered, the forces looking for comprehensive relations between the two countries got emboldened to help charter newer course of interactions between the two. Here, the credit must also be given to the top political leadership of the two countries, particularly the Japanese Prime Minister Shinzo Abe who visualised unlimited scope and avenues of close relations between the two countries. Hence, once a new script for Indo-Japan strategic ties started being written, there was no looking back. Even the sectors which were perceived to be bottlenecks for the two, have now been converted into sectors of proactive cooperation. At the same time, the unconventional aspects of their relations such as counterterrorism also gained prominence given their propensity to cause massive devastation in each of the countries. Though economic relations have been and will remain the pivot of Indo-Japan strategic ties, the significance of the perspective of international terrorism must not be underestimated. Peaceful conditions are considered as the precondition for economic prosperity in any country. Therefore, for both the countries that remain prime targets for the international terrorist organisations, it becomes critical to forge strategic collaboration to take on the bull by the horn. Fortunately, the nature of such collaboration has not just remained confined to bilateral exchanges, but has also become multilateral whose net result might be seen in the adoption of a comprehensive convention on counterterrorism by the United Nations in the near future.

Notes

1. Yoichi Funabashi, 'India and Japan: A New Strategic Affinity', *Journal of the United Service Institution of India*, (New Delhi), Vol. CXXXIV, no. 556, April-June 2004, p. 198.
2. Yasukuni Enoki, 'The Japan-India New Partnership', *Journal of the United Service Institution of India*, (New Delhi), Vol. CXXXIV, no. 557, July-September 2004, p. 325.
3. *Ibid.*
4. For an in-depth analysis of the changing politico-strategic landscape of the Asia-Pacific region and its implications for major countries, mainly India, see A.N. Ram, 'Evolving Strategic Architecture in Asia-Pacific Region: Implications for India', *Journal of the United Service Institution of India,* (New Delhi) Vol. CXXXVII, no. 569, July-September 2007, pp. 340-347. Also, see, Brahma Chellaney, 'Differential Equations', *Hindustan Times* (New Delhi), 12 February 2008, p. 12.
5. Yumi Hiwatari, 'Transformation of Japanese Security', in N.S. Sisodia and G.V.C. Naidu, eds., *India-Japan Relations: Partnership for Peace and Security in Asia,* (New Delhi: Promilla and Co., 2006), p. 15.
6. Rajiv Sikri, 'Inaugural Address', in N.S. Sisodia and G.V.C. Naidu eds., *op. cit.*, p. 4.
7. Geethanjali Nataraj, 'Japanese Investment in India: Trends and Prospects', *Economic and Political Weekly,* Vol. XLV, no. 10, March 6, 2010, p. 20.
8. G.V.C. Naidu, 'New Dimensions in the India-Japan Strategic Partnership: Shinzo Abe's Visit', *Strategic Analysis*, (New Delhi) Vol. 31, no, 6, November 2007, p. 967.
9. See, Aakriti Tandon, 'India's foreign Policy Priorities and the Emergence of a Modi Doctrine', *Strategic Analysis,* Vol. 40, no. 5, 2016, pp. 349-356.
10. For a critical overview of the Act East Policy, see, Lavina Lee, 'India as a nation of consequence in Asia: The potential and limitations of India's Act

East Policy', *The Journal of East Asian Affairs,* Vol. 29, no. 2, Fall/Winter 2015, pp. 67-104, available at http://www.jstor.org/stable/43685236, accessed on 10 October, 2017.

11. Indrani Bagchi, 'Ghost Wars: China's lengthening shadow over Asia can be countered with an India-Japan-Australia-US quadrilateral', *The Times of India,*(New Delhi), November 4, 2017, p. 22.
12. Avinash K. Dixit and Barry J. Nalebuff, *Thinking Strategically: The Competitive Edge in Business, Politics and Everyday Life,* (New York: W.W. Norton & Company, 1991), pp. 1-2.
13. P. R. Kumaraswamy, 'Redefining 'Strategic' Cooperation', *Strategic Analysis,* Vol. 41, no. 4, 2017, pp. 355-368.
14. Cf, Vivek Pinto, 'A Strategic Partnership between India and Japan?', *Economic and Political Weekly,* Vol. 40, no. 52, December 30, 2007, pp. 5299-5301.
15. In writing this section, the author has drawn liberally on the ideas presented in Yoichi Funabashi, 'India and Japan: A New Strategic Affinity' *Journal of the United Service Institution of India, op. cit.*
16. A phrase coined by the former National Security Advisor to the US President Jimmy Carter, Zbigniew Brezenski, the '*global Balkans*' refers to the stretch of land lying between the Suez Canal in the West to Russia's borders of Kazakhstan in the east. See Yoichi Funabashi, 'India and Japan: A New Strategic Affinity', *op. cit.*, pp. 199-200.
17. Gurpreet S. Khurana, 'Security of Sea Lines: Prospects of India-Japan Cooperation', *Strategic Analysis*, (New Delhi), Vol. 31, no. 1, January 2007, p. 142.
18. See, Vinay Kaura, 'India-Japan Relations and Asia's Emerging Geopolitics', *Indian Journal of Asian Affairs,* Vol. 29, no. 1 /2, June-December 2016, pp. 17-38, available at, http://www.jstor.org/stable/44123127, accessed on 6 October, 2017.
19. A. S. Narang, 'Introduction', in A.S. Narang and Pramila Srivastava, eds., *Terrorism: The Global Perspective*, (New Delhi: Kanishka Publishers, 2000), p. 3.
20. Christopher C. Harmon, *Terrorism Today*, (London: Frank Cass, 2000), p.158.
21. Brahma Chellaney, 'Fighting Terrorism in Southern Asia', *International Security,* Vol. 26, no. 3, (Winter 2001/02), p.102.
22. Mohammed Badrul Alam, 'Perceptions of Japanese Students on Terrorism and Other Security Problems: Initial Results from a Pilot Study', *Strategic Analysis,* (New Delhi), Vol. 27, no. 2, April-June 2003, pp. 279-291.
23. Masahiro Akiyama, 'Development of the Japan-US Alliance after 11 September 2001 and the war in Iraq', *Journal of the United Service*

Institution of India, (New Delhi), Vol. CXXXIII, no. 553, July-September 2003, p. 355.

24. See, Suchit Bunbongkarn, 'Non-Traditional Security Challenges in East Asia', in N.S. Sisodia and G.V.C. Naidu, eds., *Changing Security Dynamic in Eastern Asia: Focus on Japan*, (New Delhi: IDSA, 2005), pp. 370-371.
25. Arpita Mathur, 'Japan's Response to the 11 September Crisis', *Strategic Analysis*, (New Delhi), Vol. 25, no. 8, November 2001, p. 969.
26. Madhuchanda Ghosh, 'India and Japan's Growing Synergy: From a Political to a Strategic Focus', *Asian Survey*, Vol. 48, no. 2, March-April 2008, p. 292.

Chapter - 8

Changing Dynamics of India-Japan Relations: China as a Common Factor

—Gitanjali Sinha Roy

Abstract

The purpose of this chapter is to trace China's presence as a common factor with India and Japan in the present scenario and its effects on the economic, strategic and military, territorial and maritime relations. The chapter also talks about why China's growing dominance is the reason for India and Japan's ever-growing and blossoming friendship.

Economic Relations: 'Economic strength-the power to uplift or ruin economies'

Economic relations are the backbone for the stability of any country. In the present international scenario, the economic interdependence among nations leads to stronger relations so, each country aims to have greater economic development so that it not only has economic growth and prosperity but other countries also benefit due to trade relations followed by import and export, but these economic relations also get disrupted in case of disputes among nations.

The economic ties between India and China play a major role in the bilateral relations in the world by 2020 and it has been seen that it has surged to 52 billion dollars in 2008 from 3 billion dollars in 2000. In the trade sector too, India and China are increasing three times the pace of the US-China trade and it is likely to continue to do so. It is further believed that India-China trade would be 409 billion dollars and that would surpass US-China trade by 2020. The foreign direct investments (FDI) between India and China are also supposed to grow. India is a kind-off a leader in software development and China is the leading base in the Information Technology (IT) manufacturing and this synergy could well lead to an unbeaten combination. Keeping in mind, the need for energy resources, China and India are dependent on resources of oil and gas and this makes them look for overseas oil equity and in order to get the control of the oilfield, they end up outbidding each other. Thereby, both of them should aim for a strategy based on cooperation rather than competing against each other which would help them share benefits in infrastructure costs and secure the risks.

India and China are global economies with great prospects in their bags but it is also many global implications and the major implication that they faced was the Doklam dispute which led to the escalation of tensions between the troops. Finally, both sides have decided to de-escalate the tensions by the withdrawing of troops as they realised that trade was getting affected and normalisation was essential. China's trade policies are protectionist based and China continues to benefit from it and this protectionist policy affects India's pharmaceutical sector along with the generic drugs. The trade has been skewed heavily in China's favour and if restrictions are put on the import of Chinese goods it would badly affect the Indian industries as India ends up importing more than 22 million dollars' worth of electronic goods especially cheap mobile phones and information technology products. India has been criticised for its anti-dumping duties by China and the products on which anti-dumping duty is levied are chemicals and machinery items, steel and other metals, fibres and yarn, rubber, plastic, electronics and consumer goods. The basic logic behind applying this anti-dumping duty is to be able to protect the domestic industries as they don't match the cheap prices from the Chinese products. The other reason for the imposition of unreasonable restrictions on Chinese imports is because of a contravention of the World Trade Organisation's laws (WTO) and the local manufacturers in India aren't able to supply goods to the telecom sectors and developing countries and thereby, India is forced to import goods from

USA and Europe at a prohibitive cost. China is the largest trading partner of India as their bilateral trade is of 71.5 billion dollars and the total imports that India took from China last year leads to 61.3 billion dollars and the total that India exports to China is about 10.2 billion dollars, the figures of import and export between China and India gives it away that China benefits from this relationship. One needs to understand the logic behind this unfavourable trade balance between China and India is because India exports only the raw materials like copper and iron ore and the deficit can only be reduced when India starts adding the value to its exporting products but it doesn't happen because the Indian manufacturing industries sector have to develop a long way to be able to reach Chinese value added export products. India is facing problems because of Chinese cheap goods and it is affecting the 'Make in India' initiative but since the Indian market is so dependent on the Chinese goods, one can't even think of boycotting the Chinese goods.

Japan and China's economic relationship is rather crucial for the East Asian region, so it is necessary to scrutinise it well in order to understand this complex relationship. Japan roughly imported 161 billion dollars' worth of goods from China which is 27 per cent making China their top import partner in the present time. On the other hand, China has imported 116 billion dollars' worth of goods from Japan and China exports 153 billion dollars' worth of products leading to a total of 6.4 per cent. China is a more sort after trade partner as it is a consumer market which supplies products at a cheaper price and thereby, making China the sort after trade partner. Reports suggest that a new trend has emerged in the cross-border e-commerce and according to Japan's Ministry of Economy, Trade and Industry (METI), China is going to make more purchases from Japan of about 1.337 trillion Yen in 2017 and by 2020, it would be 1.905 trillion Yen.This year 2017 marks the "45th anniversary of normalisation of ties and the 40th anniversary of the signing of the Treaty of Peace and Friendship between Japan and China" and it is believed that Japan has been making many efforts for rapprochement with China and under this, the Abe administration has decided to be a part of the Belt and Road Initiative (B&RI) and further, considered joining the Asian Infrastructure Investment Bank (AIIB). One needs to realise that it is the Abe administration that is making all the efforts and it's a big indication that despite all the misbehaviour by China, Japan has taken the initiative to melt the ice yet again.

The section gives us an excellent insight into the economic ties that India and Japan share with China where it is visibly clear China has its interest in mind of being a consumer market and by supplying cheap products to the Indian and Japanese economy, it is making sure that these countries remain dependent on them and import trade continues as well and thereby, all this is benefitting China which would ultimately make them into a strong power rather a hegemonic power and this is a cause of concern for India and Japan. Further, Japan and India believe that in order to deal with China as a hegemonic power both these countries have aimed to work towards building their economies together and Japan has invested over 25 billion dollars from 2000 to 2017 in the different sectors of India. Japan is the third largest investor in India and Japan has pledged to invest 35 billion up to the period of 2014 to 2019. This clearly gives us an insight into the efforts made by India and Japan to counter and contain China.

Strategic and Military Relations: 'Subduing the enemy without a war'

Every country needs to have a strategy in place to be able to deal with their enemies and for this purpose; a military comes into play which strategically hits out in the name of national interest and states sovereignty and this is incomplete without having strategic relations in place.

India and China have a long history of wars but all that needs to kept aside and they should aim for the betterment of their strategic and military relations keeping the ever-changing relations in the international arena. Both the countries last year had their sixth chapter of joint Military Training Exercise 'Hand in Hand' with the aim to focus on transnational terrorism and counter-terrorism operations in semi-urban scenarios. India has been very supportive in getting China into the United Nations especially in the United Nations Security Council (UNSC) and thereby, India feels that China too would support its case. The irony is that in the present scenario China has been objecting to India's place in the UNSC and it has happened twice last year. China needs to realise that if India gets a membership into UNSC, it would help Asia's clout in the international affairs, but China doesn't see that as it is only bothered in building itself as a 'hegemonic power in Asia', increasing its 'China clout in the world' and it feels that if India get this UNSC seat, it would be a threat to China's dominance and thereby, China feels India needs to be pushed down and countered. Talking of counter, China and India both need to counter-terrorism as South Asia is a hub of terrorism and in the recent BRICS-Xiamen Declaration, China spoke about security issues and discussed about terrorist groups like Taliban, ISIL/DAISH, Pakistan based Al-Qaida and its affiliates including Eastern Turkistan Islamic Movement, Islamic Movement of Uzbekistan, the Haqqani network, Lashkar-e-Taiba, Jaish-e-Mohammad, TTP and Hizbut-Tahrir and it is rather interesting as it tests China's support to Pakistan at time, when Pakistan has been cornered not only in BRICS Summit hosted by China but also, at the recent United Nations General Assembly (UNGA) meeting in 2017 where India has declared Pakistan a "pure land of Terrorism called Pakistan as Terroristan" leaving Pakistan isolated but despite this China is Pakistan's all-weather friend.

The cause of concern in the relationship between India and China is China is an 'all-weather friend' of Pakistan and India is rather convinced that China has helped Pakistan by giving them access to nuclear warhead designs, fissile material and missile technology, fully assembled and crated M-9 and M-11 missiles to Pakistan. They have also been given joint weapons and equipment for developmental programmes which include Al Khalid tanks, F-22 frigates and FC-1/JF-17 fighter aircraft. India, further believes that Chinese have increased their military aid to Pakistan and helped Pakistan waging a proxy war in Jammu and Kashmir. Further, China has been constantly after India whether in the name of opposing India's nuclear weapons programme to stopping India's from joining the Nuclear Suppliers Group (NSG), to building infrastructure under string of pearls theory in and around the Indian Ocean region (IOR) to increasing activity in the Bay of Bengal to attempts to isolate India in the ASEAN Regional Forum (ARF) to being suspicious of India wanting to join the quadrilateral grouping with Japan, US and Australia and feels that the US-India strategic partnership is a way to gang up against China.

What China needs to realise that China's friendship with Pakistan is a way to gang up against India and India in order to protect her national interest and sovereignty would also need to find friends in Japan, Australia and US to gang up against China.

Japan's relation with China has been through many ups and downs especially till 2005 and the 'ice-breaking' of this relationship came with Prime Minister Shinzo Abe's visit with an aim to have "a mutually beneficial relationship based on common strategic interests", increase corporation on economic and environmental policies, find solutions to disputed areas and also deal with North Korea as it is a major cause of concern for Japan and China has good relations, but with the recent missiles being fired even China has condemned North Korea. Japan has concentrated its focus on the increasing influence of China's dominance in the Asia-Pacific region. China has made efforts towards Japan along with the Association of Southeast Asian Nations (ASEAN) including a China-ASEAN free trade agreement but it only gave rise to China's hegemony making Japan vary of China's actual intentions and created underlined level of competition between them. This competition was seen when China quietly build relations with African Union (AU) nations and Japan to try, but Japan wasn't successful the way China is. In the recent times, Japan has urged China to be more transparent with their military expansion especially after President Xi Jinping announced China's goal of becoming a strong power. Japan further asked China to explain its ballooning military expenses, naval and maritime expansion and aviation activities near Japan. China to answer Japan's questions has said that their relationship would remain on the path of peaceful development in the terms of defence policy. Though, both Japan and China have decided to work on the implementation of a maritime hotline to avoid any clashes in the East China Sea (EAS) and further agreed to start maritime and aerial communication mechanism. This year marks the 45th anniversary of the normalisation of diplomatic ties between Japan and China which is an excellent example of mutual understanding despite having so many disputes.

This section saw that China is a major cause of concern for India and Japan as China is trying very hard to build itself as a strong power not only in the Asia-Pacific region but also in the Indo-Pacific region strategically by using its string of pearls theory and expansionist policy and that has inevitably unnerved both India and Japan which has led both India and Japan aim for an ever blossoming relationship. With this new friendship blossoming since 2007, it has made many efforts to counter and contain China strategically by putting up the Asia-Africa Growth Corridor (AAGC) as a counter to China's One Belt One Road (OBOR) which is a major change in the international scenario and thus could well be the foundation for a new power order to counter China.

Territorial Relations: 'All eyes on the borders'

India and China have a long history of territorial disputes and it happens because of China's expansionist policy. This present section will deal with Aksai Chin dispute, MacMohan Line dispute, the China-Pakistan Economic Corridor (CPEC) which passes through India's disputed territory Gilghit-Baltistan and the recent Doklam dispute.

Aksai Chin is one of the most strategically important areas of dispute between India and China. India after independence used the Johnson Line which made Aksai Chin an area of Ladakh in Jammu and Kashmir but China claims it to be a part of their territory. The dispute arose in the 1950's when China build a road connecting the Xinjiang area to Tibet with a route into Aksai Chin and India wasn't aware that this road had been made until it was declared in the newspaper and maps by China. This area holds a strategic importance as it is closer to Delhi and could be seen as an immediate threat to India's sovereignty and Aksai Chin acts like an unmanned Chinese satellite which would help China keep an eye on India easily. This has always been a major cause of concern for India as it has had to increase its defence spending as well as a strengthening of borders security. India's other cause of concern is that China is Pakistan's all-weather friend and in case of a war, Pakistan might have Aksai Chin as its base which would make it very difficult for India. Aksai Chin is a natural barrier between India and China and if it was in the hands of India, it would help expose China's vulnerabilities.

The other dispute between India and China is due to the Macmohan Line, though China has never accepted this line drawn by the British India and Tibet as it believes it's a violation of their rights. China believes in the Line of Actual Control (LAC) which also sees Arunachal Pradesh as its territory and doesn't accept the Macmohan Line. India on the other hand, doesn't accept the LAC as it believes that Arunachal Pradesh is its own territory. Over the years, many times, both the countries have come to talks but haven't yet reached a solution.

India is a common enemy in the eyes of China and Pakistan and they both feel the need to counter India. With help of the One Belt One Road (OBOR), they believe it would be possible. This OBOR initiative is done by China and it aims to open up an economic trade route which would help connect Asia, Africa, the Middle East and Europe. Under this Belt and Road Initiative (B&RI), the flagship project is the China and Pakistan Economic Corridor (CPEC) which aims at a comprehensive and substantive bilateral cooperation between China and Pakistan and the initiative for this had been proposed by Chinese Premier Li Keqiang in May 2013 during his visit to Pakistan and in July 2013, the then Prime Minister of Pakistan, Nawaz Sharif signed an MOU to start work on CPEC. The central feature of the CPEC is based on the key areas like Gwadar port, energy, transportation infrastructure and industrial cooperation. Though, India has raised an objection to this project as it runs through the Gilgit-Baltistan which is situated in the north-western corner of Jammu and Kashmir. As India sees the Gilgit-Baltistan area as a part of the Indian Territory and claims that it has been illegally occupied by Pakistan, thereby, it is seen as an insensitive move on India's sovereignty and territorial integrity and India feels that they have never been fully explained or told about the Road and Belt Initiative (R&BI). Further, this project can't just be seen from an economic project perspective and it should also be seen from a political perspective with an aim to have control promoted by China. Further, this project should be seen as China's neo-colonial policy where smaller countries induced into the debt cycle, their ecology destroyed and result in the disruption of local communities and inhabitants. Thereby, India had refused to attend the OBOR conference organised by China and the refusal to attend this conference came after a year's bilateral discord as China opposed India's entry into the Nuclear Suppliers Group (NSG) already twice last year. Though, the road ahead would only become tougher as India is also the co-founder of the Asian Infrastructural Investment Bank (AIIB) and has recently become a member of the Shanghai Cooperation Organisation (SCO) from June 2017 and both these organisations would ask India to support the B&RI project which would only make it a very difficult situation as the UN Secretary-General has given an endorsement mentioning the B&RI to be seen from the perspective of a shared vision aimed at global development and with India sitting out of this conference would ultimately deny itself an unending benefit which got come its way.

Prior to this, the Tibetan Spiritual leader Dalai Lama had visited Arunachal Pradesh and was later hosted by the then President of India Pranab Mukherjee and all this didn't go down well with the Chinese. The Chinese reacted in an unexpected manner by stopping the Indian pilgrims to go to Kailash Mansarovar by the Nathu La pass in Sikkim and this was the starting of the recent standoff. The recent face-off between India-China resulted in a tri-junction between India, Bhutan and China in Doklam, Sikkim and the cause for this face-off was the opposition by the Indian troops on the construction of the road by the Chinese in the Doklam plateau. This road became a major concern for India because this road if completed would shorten the distance between China and India's strategically vulnerable 'Chicken Neck' area also called the Siliguri Corridor and it further, extends from Darjeeling, Jalpaiguri and Terai regions of West Bengal towards the Northeast and it becomes a rail hub connecting the military formations along the Line of Actual Control (LAC) and road network for connecting to West Bengal and the Northeastern states. Siliguri Corridor is essential as it joins the Northeast to India and it lies in the Chumbi Valley of the Chinese held Tibetan Autonomous Region which is dangerous for both the Indian states of Sikkim and Arunachal Pradesh. Reports have suggested that Chinese have already build a road near Doka La and want to extend it towards Gamochen which is guarded by the Indian troops and that would mean intrusion into the Bhutan territory. The year 2007 marked the India-Bhutan Friendship Treaty and Bhutan banks on India to be protected and since Bhutan has no diplomatic ties with China so; it is a greater responsibility for India to keep this trust intact.

China is one country in the world which has a territorial dispute with almost every country. China believes in being the big daddy that can aggressively control anyone by arm-twisting and bullying. China basically suffers from a massive sense of insecurity and to feel secure it likes to have control over its neighbours and the only way they are able to fulfil this desire is by their theory of expansionism. What China doesn't realise that in the present scenario, the way the international relations are being balanced, China too will have to face the consequences of its aggressive nature if it doesn't find a balance soon and India along with Japan supported by the US could also be a good game plan to counter China and her aggressive dominance.

Maritime Relations: 'Conflict over strategic waters-Water Wars'

The future of the changing dynamics in international relations would be based on the maritime relations as it is believed that the future will be seen in the Indo-Pacific region. Thereby, the need to have control over strategic water bodies would depict the importance of a particular country at the international level and the 'future wars could be on waters'.

The Indian Ocean has strategic importance for China as it imports up to 82 per cent for its energy requirements in the form of oil and gas and 30 per cent from the sea trades and both are shipped through the Indian Ocean Region (IOR). Since China is a manufacturing hub; it automatically becomes dependent on the trade routes from the Indian Ocean and African region as they help in the supply of the 3 m's-raw materials, minerals, markets and labour. The Malacca Strait becomes a major checkpoint as the bulk of China's trade and energy passes through it and the Former President Hu Jintao spoke of the 'Malacca Dilemma' and said: "whosoever controls the Malacca Strait would end up having a control over China's energy route". China remains worried for its energy supplies and thereby, they have ventured in the Persian Gulf to help them get the supply of the energy resources like oil and natural gases and aimed to build a special relationship with these countries in the Persian Gulf. China has many guns pulled out for the 'Indian Ocean dependency' and are following the 'string of pearls theory', under which China has taken the initiative to build ports, pipelines, roadways and railways all connected to Eurasia, Africa and the Indian Ocean and the participants in these Chinese funded port building projects are Sri Lanka, Pakistan, Myanmar and countries along the East African coast. Under the One Belt One Road Initiative (OBOR), China has facilitated another project called the China-Pakistan-Economic-Corridor (CPEC) which is an initiative for China to have access to the Arabian Sea which is east of the Persian Gulf and also building deep sea ports being developed in Gwadar, Pakistan to be connected to a road-pipeline project in the Xinjiang province of China. On the other hand, China has facilitated the building of ports in Myanmar at Sittwe and Kyaukphu to railroad-waterway-pipeline facilities in Myanmar to link the Bay of Bengal to China's Yunnan province and a canal system build across the Kra Isthmus in Thailand to help increase the Chinese energy resources. Further, the Chinese have been successful in the building of additional ports with its naval facilities at Hambantota in Sri Lanka, Marao in Maldives and Kyaukphu, Hianggyi, Great Coco, Mergui and Zadetkyi in Myanmar. The intention of China was very clear in their 2015 Defence White Paper which clearly spoke about the security concerns overseas with respect to the energy resources, strategic sea lines of communication (SLOCs) and the People's Liberation Army Navy's (PLAN) gradual shift to a combination of offshore water defence with an open seas protection. China's involvement could be traced back to the time, when PLAN had participated in the multi-national anti-piracy operations off the Horn of Africa's to building a military base in Djibouti to docking submarines in the Colombo and Karachi to finally building a long-standing partnership with Pakistan to add value to their naval power and move towards becoming a 'naval hegemonic power' in this region.

India's interest in the Indian Ocean is obvious as the Indian Ocean is India's own baby and about 70 per cent of its oil and gas are imported from the sea for India and is expected to reach an all high at 95 per cent by 2025. India's primary concern of holding the Indian Ocean is because 77 per cent of the Indian trade comes from it and as per 2007, India has become the fourth largest trading partner in the region of the Indian Ocean. India's wake-up call to China's 'geostrategic encirclement theory' also known as the 'string of pearls theory' was dealt by using the Indian Navy's 2015 maritime security strategy which covered the primary areas of interest ranging from the Cape of Good Hope to Indonesia's Lombok Straits including the Malacca Strait and this frightened the Chinese of India's naval capabilities. Chinese fear that the Indian naval capacity would be a built up of 200 ships by 2027 and the Joint Strategic Vision for Asia-Pacific and Indian Ocean Region in 2015 with the United States of America where they aimed for "safeguarding maritime security and ensuring freedom of navigation…especially in the South China Sea" and that would inevitably change the politics of the Indian Ocean. India has also strengthened her relationship with Seychelles, Mauritius, Vietnam and Sri Lanka and is working towards building a blue economy supported by projects like Sagarmala and Mausam. China further fears that India could fortify these islands of Andaman and Nicobar into a 'metal chain' that could act as a blockade against Malacca and further use the Andaman's as a strategic spring broad to push India's Look East Policy, which currently is known as the 'Act East Policy' paving way for the betterment of relations in the South China Sea (SCS).

China's maritime conflict in the South China Sea (SCS) is yet another example of China's expansionist policy as this region is a significant commercial gateway for the Indo-Pacific region and it is bordered by Brunei, Cambodia, China, Indonesia, Malaysia, Philippines, Singapore, Taiwan, Thailand and Vietnam who are the key players in this region. Japan and South Korea also heavily rely on the South China Sea for its supply of fuels, raw materials and export route. Despite the signing of the United Nations Convention on the Law of the Sea (UNCLOS), China and Philippines along with Taiwan, Vietnam, and Malaysia have been conflicting on disputes over the Spratly, Paracel and Scarborough Shoal Islands. China has made the largest claim in the South China Sea with the dash line. China has been notoriously being aggressive in this area by starting drilling operations, colliding vessels leading to the sinking of a Vietnamese fishing boat to the construction and installation of large-scale military capable infrastructure to further building multiple runways and port facilities. This is a clear indication that China will do whatever it needs to in order to achieve its goal of occupying territory in the South China Sea.

East Asia Sea (EAS) is another example of China's maritime dispute based on the Daioyu Islands against Japan who call it the Senkaku Islands and this dispute has been overlapping with the exclusive economic zone (EEZ) by the United Nations Convention on the Law of the Sea (UNCLOS). China claims that the earliest record of the Daioyu Island can be traced to the book Voyage with a Tail Wind published in 1403 and the surrounding waters were used for fishing for generations and also claimed that these islands had been used by the Ming Dynasty as a coastal defence against the Japanese pirates. China claims that Japan stole these islands from them during the First Sino-Japanese War. On the contrary, Japan claims that these islands had been subsequently incorporated into the Japanese territory in 1895 after their victory in the First Sino-Japanese War and later, briefly had been incorporated in the American Occupation in 1945 and was returned to them in 1972 under the Okinawa Reversion Agreement and further, Japan claimed that neither China or Taiwan have claimed these islands earlier and it was only in 2012 that the Japanese Government bought these islands from a private Japanese owner to which China protected saying that their sovereignty had been violated. The question here arises that why are these islands so important? These islands have great economic and strategic advantages as they are near to the shipping lanes which transit international trade, a major fishing bed and also a big possibility of abundance of natural resources like oil, gas and mineral deposits. Further, the location has strategic importance due to the rise in competition amongst Japan, China and the United States of America for gaining a military supremacy in the Asia-Pacific region. China yet again is slowly but steadily violating the boundaries of this island by sending in the military as well as fishing ships into the Senkaku waters despite the fierce protects by the Japanese Government. It has been seen further both the Chinese and Taiwanese military forces have entered the areas with planes which have led the Japan Air Self-Defence Forces to scramble its jets. The other cause of conflict between Japan and China is Okinotorishima as Japan calls it an island and China calls it rocks and according to the international law, China doesn't recognise it as a surrounding 200-mile exclusive zone. For Japan, it is strategically important as it uses the cultured coral reefs and plans to eventually make an island of corals. The need to solve these disputes is essential as these maritime conflicts affect the marine life, inhabitants living in and around these places and the inevitably leads to the deterioration of the environment.

This section on the maritime relations depicted a very importance and significant finding that future of international politics is in the arena of international waters and to be a leader here, China is all set to raise the bar on the maritime front despite facing so many disputes with major powers like India, China and the US. It is clear that China is aggressively following an expansionist policy not only on land but also on water as it believes that to be a maritime superpower it needs to venture out and lead in the maritime sector and that's the reason why they are building themselves into a massive naval hegemonic power accompanied by its encirclement theory which would help them keep an eye on their competitors as well. China has also realised that after the Asia-Pacific region, the Indo-Pacific region will be the next in line to be future leaders and thereby, it is also very cleverly setting its base here so that it can also be a leader in the Indo-Pacific region. What China needs to realise that both India and Japan aren't going to give China an easy run as they too have plans to counter China and contain its dominance as they too plan to be leaders in the Indo-Pacific region.

Conclusion

The purpose of this chapter was to highlight China as a common factor prevalent in the India-China and Japan-China relations and it clearly showed that both India and Japan are unhappy with the relationship that they have with China. It's due to China's aggressive nature and dominance that both India and Japan feel that China needs to be countered and contained as China as a 'hegemonic power' is a major threat to India as well as Japan's sovereignty. In order to deal with China, the relations between India and Japan have changed since 2007 and have been at an all high since then. In order to counter China's mischievousness in India's Northeast, Japan has set up India-Japan Cooperation Forum for Development of North East which is building in the sector of strategic infrastructure (highways and road connectivity), electricity and disaster management and this would strengthen India-Japan and Japan-Northeast relations. Further, Japan sees the development of the Northeast as an essential key to promoting India's Act East Policy as it will connect India to the Southeast Asian nations which would help build better relations with countries there and they all together will work towards countering China as one entity. Japan has been involved in the infrastructural development of the Mumbai-Ahmedabad Shinkansen high-speed rail corridor project, which is India's first bullet train project of being 19 billion dollars line, is to be functional by the end of 2023. India and Japan have an idea of paving way for a growth corridor of linking Asia and Africa had been discussed by Prime Minister Shinzo Abe and Prime Minister Narendra Modi in November 2016 and that gave birth to the "vision document on the Asia-Africa Growth Corridor (AAGC)" which aims at the development projects in health and pharmaceuticals, agriculture and agro-processing, disaster management and skill enhancement. Some believe that the Asia-Africa Growth Corridor (AAGC) is a way to counter China's One Belt One Road (OBOR) Initiative, but the reality is rather different. The AAGC is a consultative initiative which is essentially a sea project and the OBOR is a land project. Thereby, the policy applied by India and China is both different. China mostly concentrates on the infrastructure and 'cheque book diplomacy' and India on the other hand, aims for cooperation projects and programmes focussed on the development of African human resources. In the military sector, the Malabar exercises held with India, Australia, Japan and US being a part of it clearly shows a military grouping ready to counter China's wrong intentions. The recent visit of US Secretary of State, Rex Tillerson suggested that Washington along with India should together build roads and ports across South Asia to Asia-Pacific in response to China's OBOR and also said that US along with India, Japan and Australia should be four anchors of security and peace in the Indo-Pacific region and this clearly signifies that China is indeed being countered and contained by a group of future leaders ready to take China on. This could well be a foundation for a new era moving towards a big strategic picture with an aim of an open ocean, better economy and stable and reliable security.

References

Bhatia, Rajiv. (2017). *Opinion: The time for Africa* dated June 1st, 2017 in *the Hindu.*(Accessed on 1st June, 2017).

Chaudhary, Shantanu Roy. (2016). *The Senkaku Islands Dispute* in *International Policy Digest* dated 1st August, 2016. URL: https://intpolicydigest.org/2016/08/01/senkaku-islands-dispute/.(Accessed on 26th October, 2017).

Chellaney, Brahma. (2015). *China's Indian Ocean Strategy.*URL: https://www.japantimes.co.jp/opinion/2015/06/23/commentary/world-commentary/chinas-indian-ocean-strategy/#.WdvG-WiCxPY.(Accessed on 2nd October, 2017).

Dasgupta, Saibal. (2017). *China wants India to go slow on Asia-Africa corridor.*| TNN|Updated: September 3, 2017, 02:21 IST.URL: http://times of india.indiatimes.com/world/china/china-tries-to-dilute-africa-growth-initiative-crafted-by-india japan/articleshow/60341683.cms.(Accessed on 6th September, 2017).

Dutta, Anushree. (2017). *Doklam Standoff: China's Border Provocation in India and Bhutan* published on July 13, 2017. URL: http://www.claws.in/1773/doklam-standoff-china%E2%80%99s-border-provocation-in-india-and-bhutan-anushree-dutta.html.(Accessed on 4th August, 2017).

Farley, Robert. (2016). *Can the PLA Navy Make the Indian Ocean Chinese? Does China need to dominate the Indian Ocean in order to have a world-class navy?* Dated on 1st February, 2016.(Accessed on 15th October, 2017).

Gupta, Anil Kumar and Haiyan Wang.(2009). *China and India: Greater Economic Integration* in the *China Business Review* dated 1st September, 2009. URL:https://www.chinabusinessreview.com/china-and-india-greater-economic-integration/.(Accessed on 3oth October, 2017).

Joshi, Manoj. (2017). *Doklam: To Start at the Very Beginning*-ORF Special Report. Published by *2017 Observer Research Foundation.*URL: http://www.orfonline.org/research/doklam-start-very-beginning/.(Accessed on 30th October, 2017).

Kanwal, Gurmeet. (2010). *India-China Strategic Relations-Further Improvement is Contingent on Resolution of the Territorial Dispute* in *Claws Journal* l: Summer 2010 published by Centre for Land Warfare Studies, New Delhi. URL: http://www.claws.in/images/journals_doc/1397629357Gurmeet%20Kanwal%20CJ%20Summer%202010.pdf.(Accessed on 29th October, 2017).

Osti, Donatello. (2013). *The Historical Background to Territorial Dispute over the Senkakau/Diaoyu Islands* in *ISPI* Analysis No. 183, June 2013. URL: http://www.ispionline.it/sites/default/files/pubblicazioni/analysis_183_2013.pdf.(Accessed on 27th October, 2017).

Przystup, James. (2012). *Japan-China Relations 2005–2010: Managing Between a Rock and a Hard Place*-An Interpretative Essay under *the Institute for*

Chapter - 9

India's Strategic Convergence with Japan: The Changing Indo-Pacific Geopolitical Context

—*Subhransu Sekhar Misra*

Lately, the geopolitical landscape in the Indo-Pacific region has undergone unprecedented changes with the rise of new powers, and the ensuing new challenges to regional security. In latest, in the changing and complex regional security environment of Asia, few relationships among the major powers have undergone such a remarkable turnaround as the relationship between India and Japan. It is evident from the India-Japan civilian nuclear cooperation agreement, Japan-India maritime security partnership, and Japan's participation in the Indo-US Malabar naval exercises are some of the major developments which have transformed their bilateral relationships in recent times. The 'Indo-Pacific' construct, which conceives the Western Pacific and the Indian Ocean as an interconnected geopolitical and economic space, has assumed key importance in the emerging geopolitics and geo-economics of Twenty-first Century Asia. One of the driving factors behind this region's growing importance is the massive movement of international trade on the Indo-Pacific sea lanes of communications (SLOCs). In this context, both India and Japan, are among the most concerned about security in the region and are also increasingly ready to work with each other on it. The relationship between the two countries has grown increasingly robust with regular high-level summit-meetings between the Japanese Prime Minister Shinzo Abe and his Indian counterpart, Mr Modi who have achieved spectacular success in terms of bilateral exchanges at diplomatic, defence, and business levels.

Lately, China's maritime assertiveness in the East and South China Seas, as well as the Indian Ocean region, and its push to expand its geopolitical influence beyond East Asia through its Belt and Road Initiative (BRI) and maritime Silk Road and Asian Infrastructure Investment Bank (AIIB) are vigorous diplomatic moves which have made Japan and India to come closer in their economic and military ties. To counter the Chinese expansionism, both India and Japan have come to share a sense of purpose in promoting the current order in the region, with the focus on transparent institutions, good governance, and international law.

Indo-Pacific Region and the Strategic Convergence of India and Japan

Historically, for the first time on August 22, 2007, the Japanese Prime Minister Shinzo Abe used the Indo-Pacific term in his address to Indian Parliament titled, "Confluence of the Two Seas" which continued as follows:

> "Now, as this new "broader Asia" takes shape at the confluence of the two seas of the Indian and Pacific Oceans, I feel that it is imperative that the democratic nations located at opposite edges of these seas deepen the friendship among their citizens at every possible level."[1]

Thus, Japan seeks for a free and open Indo-Pacific strategy with India through enhancing maritime security cooperation, improving connectivity in the wider Indo-Pacific region and strengthening cooperation with the ASEAN as a whole. This has been widely reflected in the enhancement of defence and security cooperation and dialogues, including the MALABAR and other joint exercises, defence equipment and technology cooperation in such areas as surveillance and unmanned system technologies, and military cooperation. Thus, the Indo-Pacific region is on a threshold of a major change as India and Japan propose the creation of a sea-corridor, the Asia-Pacific Growth Corridor (AAGC), linking the two continents, Asia and Africa, as an alternative to China's maritime Silk Road. AAGC reflects the growing strategic convergence of India and Japan over the issue of promoting freedom of navigation in the Indo-Pacific region. Both states have reasons to support freedom of navigation in the Indo-Pacific—including the South China Sea—to safeguard the maritime commons stretching from the Indian Ocean region to the Pacific and together contribute toward maintaining the regional balance of power. The common strategic interests and concerns have propelled Prime Minister Abe to dub Japan and India as natural allies for their faith in democratic culture. With both the Prime Minister Abe and Modi having good personal chemistry, India-Japan strategic engagement will have a decisive impact on the Asian balance of power in terms of peace and order in the Indo-Pacific region. In this context, it is pertinent to examine the role of various actors in the Indo-Pacific region in view of their strategic and military interests.

Rise of China and US Pivot to Asia-Pacific : Japanese Perspectives

In the post-Cold War scenario, with decline in Russian influence in global affairs, the US has maintained its presence as a 'resident' Power in the Asia–Pacific, where it has continued its role as 'net security provider' by ensuring a stable and peaceful regional order in which Asian nations have been able to rise and prosper. But with a rising China with its hegemonic ambitions in the South China Sea, the maritime disputes have brought together US, Japan, Australia and India together under a common platform of democratic alliance to maintain rule-based order in the Asia-Pacific region.

Therefore, on November 2011, US President Barack Obama in his address to the Australian Parliament announced a new policy, "US Rebalance to the Asia–Pacific", as he flagged his plan to consolidate and magnify the American presence in the region, signaling a shift in America's regional strategic focus from the Middle East and Europe to East and South Asia. Obama affirmed 'The United States is a Pacific power, and we are here to stay.'[2] There is wider consensus among the strategic experts that China has become the dominant economic power in Asia, and it is seeking to translate that power, through an activist foreign policy, into geopolitical influence and a new global order.[3] On the back of phenomenal economic growth, China is pursuing its ambitions to modernise its military and establish a sphere of influence in the Asia–Pacific. Presently, the 'peaceful rise' advocated by Hu Jintao has been transformed under the leadership of Xi Jinping, who has pursued a more muscular foreign policy since taking office in 2013. The examples are numerous: the unilateral declaration of an air defence identification zone over a large area of the East China Sea, the installation of a state-owned oil rig in Vietnam's exclusive economic zone, the occupation of Scarborough Shoal (claimed by the Philippines) and the frenetic land reclamation efforts to transform reefs and rocks in the South China Sea into islands complete with airstrips, ports and buildings. In an effort to reform the regional order and upset the status quo, China is challenging international rules and global norms through a coercive, provocative and damaging campaign that continues to raise tensions and unsettle many in the region and beyond. China's rise is America's central strategic challenge, and Beijing's increasing bellicosity and brinksmanship are of great concern to its Asia–Pacific neighbours.[4]

In recent times, China's rise and the relative decline of US power in the Asia–Pacific have done much to shape Japan's conception of, and response to, the increasingly complex regional threat environment. After long years of pacifist tradition, the present Prime Minister Shinzô Abe has stated that Japan's foreign policy priority must be to expand the country's strategic horizons with the 'assertion and affirmation of Japan's global status as a "first-tier nation". Beyond his domestic focus on reinvigorating the long-stagnant Japanese economy, Abe has energetically pursued a global yet Asia-focused agenda with such initiatives as the 'Arc of Freedom and Prosperity', 'Proactive Contribution to Peace' and 'Asia's Democratic Security Diamond'.[5] This agenda is based on an understanding that China remains Japan's main strategic competitor and threat since both are in dispute over the Senkaku/ Diaoyu Islands in the East China Sea. This has reinforced Abe's activism that has lifted Japan's self-imposed ban on arms exports. Under Abe, Japan has seen three consecutive years of increased defence spending—although, at a modest one per cent of GDP, reversing the earlier trends. Most significant, however, have been Abe's efforts to normalise Japan's military posture and power by reinterpreting the constraints imposed by Article 9 of the Japanese Constitution.

Japan has also taken the lead in initiating multilateral agenda like the Quadrilateral Security Dialogue involving the US, Australia and India which would permit Japan to play a more active and 'seamless' security role in the region and be better able to defend itself and its allies and with his re-election as PM in October, 2017 for a five year term, Abe has the political stability to continue his ambitious domestic agenda, redefine Japan's role in the world and confirm his country's commitment to proactive pacifism and multilateralism.[6]

On the other hand, the Chinese strategy against India has three elements like encirclement, envelopment and entanglement to limit the latter's power projection at regional level.[7] Globally, China hardened its stance on India's membership to the Nuclear Suppliers Group (NSG) and UN Security Council (UNSC). India countered China by deciding not to endorse China's 'Belt and Road Initiative' despite repeated overtures from China. In response, the Modi government has sought to establish closer relations with the US and Japan as it signed the logistics agreement (LEMOA for naval interoperability) with the US in 2016 and has continued with the Malabar military exercises involving India, Japan and the US. Also New Delhi has rejuvenated its 'Act East' policy by closer engagement with the ASEAN and Australia.[8]

India and Japan: Growing Closer Ties

In December 2006, Abe and the then Prime Minister of India, Dr Manmohan Singh, signed the Joint Statement Towards Japan–India Strategic and Global Partnership, establishing a deeper relationship with a strategic dimension and an upward trajectory. Later in August 2007, Abe visited Delhi for a historic address to the Indian Parliament on the 'Confluence of the Two Seas'—Pacific and Indian Oceans of freedom and of prosperity'. He set out a new vision for Japan–India relations as a positive contributor to a 'broader Asia' on the basis of shared values and strategic interests. In September 2014, Abe and Modi upgraded bilateral ties to a Special Strategic and Global Partnership—a testament to growing affinities and concerns and aligned values and ambitions. The Japanese and Indian foreign ministers continue to convene an Annual Strategic Dialogue, as do the Japanese and Indian Defence Ministers. Japan and India continue to hold an annual 2+2 meeting of Foreign and Defence Secretaries, for a healthy exchange of ideas.

Thus, Japan seeks for a free and open Indo-Pacific strategy with India through enhancing maritime security cooperation, improving connectivity in the wider Indo-Pacific region and strengthening cooperation with the ASEAN as a whole. This has been widely reflected in the enhancement of defence and security cooperation and dialogues, including the MALABAR and other joint exercises, defence equipment and technology cooperation in such areas as surveillance and unmanned system technologies, and military cooperation.

India's Policy of 'Look East' to 'Act East' and Indian Ocean Region

If one makes a broad assessment of India's diplomatic and strategic moves since its independence, India has largely overlooked the importance of the region to its East till 1990s. Broadly referred as Indo-China, this region of Southeast Asia stretching from Myanmar on India's border to Indonesia has great geopolitical and cultural affinity with the Indian subcontinent which was the fulcrum of the Indian Ocean region. It was only in 1992, under Prime Minister Narasimha Rao, India officially initiated its Look East policy—a deliberate attempt to bring India closer to economically dynamic Southeast Asia which was largely referred as region of 'Asian Tigers' for their rapid economic development pursuing free-market economic model. As a multilateral trade organisation, the Association of Southeast Asian Nations or the ASEAN invited India to play a strong role in order to balance China which had an overarching presence in the region. So in 1996, India became a full dialogue member of the ASEAN and a member in the ASEAN Regional Forum (ARF). These developments formalised and institutionalised India's Look East policy with stronger involvement in Southeast Asia in terms of economic and cultural ties with the countries in the region. This is evident from the Annual Report of 1997/1998 of The Ministry of Defence which stated that when it comes to India's security interests beyond the Indian Ocean Region, India's new broader security horizon includes 'countries of ASEAN, Central Asia, the Gulf regions, and the Indian Ocean community.'[9]

However, there are several factors which have stirred India towards a more comprehensive maritime policy in view of the Chinese build-up in Indian Ocean littorals in terms of development of infrastructure and port facilities to bolster its naval presence. So the Chinese economic investment and bulid-up of port facilities in Sitttwe in Mynmar, Humbantota in southern Sri Lanka, and Chittagong in Bangladesh and Gwadar in Pakistan has been considered as its 'Sring of Pearls' strategy to contain India in the Indian Ocean region.[10] Moreover, the latest maritime Silk Road and OBOR project for growing cooperation with Indian Ocean littoral nations as well as its rapid expansion of the blue water navy have stirred New Delhi to strengthen its maritime capability in the Indian Ocean considered to be its 'strategic backyard'. Another motivation to play a significant role in the Indo-Pacific region has come from the concerns of a 'Rising China' which is shared by regional powers like the United States, Australia and Japan in the context of a quadrilateral maritime co-operation. In this context, it is pertinent to examine India's strategic concerns in view of its 'Act East' policy covering the Indian Ocean Region and extending up to the West Pacific Ocean.

Gradually, the maritime presence of Major Powers in Indian Ocean security threat perception the Indian Ocean region received more attention from policy-makers in Delhi for its strategic importance. India could realise that India should not and cannot ignore that it has a coastline of 7,500 km and is surrounded by oceans and seas in three sides of its international boundaries. As far as the Indian Ocean is concerned, its various channels are responsible for two-thirds of world's oil shipment, one-third of world's cargo movement and nearly half of its container traffic. Moreover, the success of increasing number of regional trading blocs across the world played a stimulator for India's integration with various regional groupings. Given this context, India sought to articulate its interests in multilateral bodies like the Indian Ocean Rim-Association for Regional Cooperation (IOR-ARC) which is presently known as Indian Ocean Rim Association- IORA) and Indian Ocean Naval Symposium. So lately, India has pursued a vigorous policy of engagement in the Indian Ocean as is evident from the words of our Prime Minister Mr. Modi:

> "For us, it also serves as a strategic bridge with the nations in our immediate and extended maritime neighbourhood. In March last year in Mauritius, I had spelt out our vision for the Indian Ocean. The Indian Ocean Region is one of my foremost policy priorities. Our approach is evident in our vision of 'SAGAR' which means ocean and stands for Security and Growth for all in the Region."[11]

During his 2015 visit to Mauritius and Seychelles, Prime Minister Mr. Modi underlined that India is now ready to mark its presence in the wider geographic region of the Indo-Pacific and India may even consider building military bases outside its own national territory. In order to garner regional cooperation in enhancing maritime security, at Mauritius, PM Modi said,

> "Our goal is to seek a climate of trust and transparency; respect for international maritime rules and norms by all countries; sensitivity to each other's interests; peaceful resolution of maritime security issues; and increase in maritime cooperation."

Thus, India's new vision for maritime security is comprehensively articulated by the Indian Navy in 2015 in the document, *Ensuring Secure Seas: Indian Maritime Security Strategy*. The document clarifies that the Indian Navy's interest areas now cover the Red Sea, Gulf of Oman, Gulf of Aden, IOR island nations, Southwest Indian Ocean and East Coast of Africa littoral countries among many other nations and areas. Moreover, the South China Sea, East China Sea and Western Pacific Ocean and their littoral nations are included in the Indian Navy's secondary priority areas.

From this it is obvious that New Delhi is trying to play a constructive role in the ASEAN region which advocates for a larger Indian role in South China Sea on the one hand and on the other, the Pacific rim countries like the US, Australia and Japan want to see India as a net security provider in the Indian Ocean. The Joint Strategic Vision with the US and Japan's inclusion into the Malabar Exercise, bilateral exchanges with countries like Japan, Australia and Indonesia and re-engaging with the Indian Ocean Region (IOR) and South Pacific island nations–all signal India's preparedness for a critical role in the

Indo-Pacific region. In this light, India has embarked on indigenisation of defence capabilities, diversifying sources for its naval hardware, increasing number of joint exercises with IOR partner countries, blue economy and sustainable use of marine resources in a co-operative manner.

In his last visit to India, the Japanese Prime Minister Shinzo Abe has said: "A strong India leads to a strong Japan, and a strong Japan leads to a strong India," underscoring the necessity of India-Japan relations for the peace and stability of the Indo-Pacific region. Japan also has acknowledged India's long tradition of credible practice of democratic values and its commitment towards the freedom of navigation which makes India a suitable strategic partner of Japan. Hence, the strong security relationship between these Asiatic giants can play a crucial role in framing the security architecture and will define the stability of the rule-based global order of the newly evolved strategic geography of the Indo-Pacific.

References

1. Ministry of Foreign Affairs of Japan, *'Confluence of the two seas*—Speech by H.E. Mr Shinzo Abe, Prime Minister & David Brewster (2010), 'The India–Japan Security Relationship: An Enduring Security Partnership', Asian Security, Vol. 6, No. 2 (2010), pp. 95-120
2. B. Obama, 'Remarks by President Obama to the Australian Parliament', Parliament House, Canberra, Australia, 17 November 2011.
3. Ashley J. Tellis (2013), "Balancing without Containment: A US Strategy for Confronting China's Rise", The Washington Quarterly, Vol. 36, No. 4, pp. 109-24.
4. K Rudd, 'Xi Jinping: China's strong hand', Time, 16 April 2015 & Charles Glaser (2011), "Will China's Rise lead to War?", Foreign Affairs, Vol. 90, No. 2, March/April 2011, pp. 80-91.
5. Abe, Shinzo (2012), 'Asia's Democratic Security Diamond', Project Syndicate, 27 December 2012.
6. Stephen R.Nagy (2017), "Japan's Proactive Pacifism: Investing in Multilateralization and Omnidirectional Hedging", Strategic Analysis, Vol. 41, No. 3, pp. 223-235 & H. V. Pant, (2017), 'India, Japan, Australia, and the US: the return of Asia's Quad', The Diplomat, 28 April 2017.
7. Mohan Malik (2011), China and India: Great Power Rivals, Boulder, CO, London: First Forum Press, p. 9.

8. C. Raja Mohan (2015), Modi's World: Expanding India's Sphere of Influence (New Delhi: Harper Collins) p. 133.
9. Ministry of Defence, Govt. of India, Annual Report, 1997-1998, p. 2.
10. Shashank Joshi (2011), "Why India is Becoming Warier of China", Current History, 110(735), April, 2011, pp. 156-161.

Chapter - 10

Asian; ASEAN and Indo-Japan Economic Engagement: A Neoclassicism Perspective

—*R. P. Pradhan*

Introduction

Contemporary Indo-Japan engagement has evolved from its civilisational and cultural boundaries to a more matured neoclassical as well as a framework of political neo-realist approach today. While the Asian and ASEAN economic globalisation facilitated a closer economic neoclassicism to guide the Indo-Japan engagement frame work post 1991, political and strategic stress building up in Asia in the last couple of years has unmistakably taken both India and Japan together into incremental strategic partnership and neorealist cooperation.

Though the political and strategic configuration in the Indo-Pacific dominates the larger contemporary foreign policy discourse today, understanding depth of Indo-Japan economic engagement is the primary motivation of this paper. However, since Indo-Japan bilateralism is heavily dominated by regional context, this paper looks at Indo-Japan economic engagement paradigm from the comparative Asian and ASEAN perspective too.

Given the regional geopolitical construct, India and Japan have been traditional friends. However, till early 1980s Indo-Japan Automobile collaborations or even till the mid 1990s, India's economic engagement with Japan primarily remained of Import Substitution (ISI) order. While the quantity of bilateral trade continues to be rather far less than potential even today, both countries have embarked on a course of economic neoclassicism is visible from the range of trade instruments, emerging picture of India favourable Terms of Trade, bilateral investments and layers of economic cooperation modules.

In the interest of simplifying Indo-Japan economic engagement paradigm, this paper deconstructs Indo-Japan engagement into a theoretical framework of neoclassicism to capture the larger gamut of political economy of Indo-Japan engagement. Using neoclassical tool, this paper shall theoretically and empirically capture and clarify the rising Indo-Japan economic bilateralism and its depth and challenges in the regional climate of economic integration models.

Neoclassicism and Asian Regional Climate

The term 'Neoclassical' was first used by American economist and sociologist Thorstein Veblen in 1900 (Hodgson, 1998). A neoclassical paradigm shifts attention to economic productivity and growth through the optimisation of capital and market forces, international investment and the institutional mechanisms to support and supplement a favourable economic climate for higher order of economic growth and productivity. While neoclassicism received further refinement through a generation of economists like Robert Solow, T.W. Swan, Harrod–Domar, John Maynard *Keynes*, Robert Gilpin and Paul Samuelson, the importance of foreign capital investment in domestic market remained underestimated till the collapse of the Soviet Union. Interestingly, soon after the collapse of Soviet Union, Import Substitution and Industrialisation (ISI) model which had dominated political economy discourse for over four decades also collapsed and along with it, the emerging South-South Cooperation also lost its steam.

Since 1991, market, capital, cross-border trade and myriad formats of market and economic integration tools theoretically referred to as economic neoclassicism overridingly penetrated into the world system. The neoclassical approach since then nearly revised many old orders and toned down the role of strategic security perception and diluted the discourse to more focus around securing market, resources, trade and investment towards economic growth and productivity (Masanori, 2012). Neoclassicism proposes economic prosperity away from zero-sum spiral of strategic insecurity competition and focus on laissez-faire, capital market, export led growth and higher role of non-state actors-phenomena of political neo-liberalism.

Within Asia, the major impetus for structural change occurred not primarily with the end of the Cold War but rather with the shift in China's economic trajectory. The Chinese leader Deng Xiaoping, influenced by the 1970s economic prosperity of Japan, Taiwan, Singapore, Hong Kong and South Korea, virtually re-scripted an Asian version of political neo-liberalism and economic neoclassicism reforms in 1978 - a crucial Chinese economic outlook and policy shift (Harvey, 2005). Chinese economic miracle opened up space to revisit and validate existing international relations theories.

What emerged from this paradigm shift is a rush for Regional Trade Agreements and market integration movement (Brown, Shaheen, *et al.,* 2005). Regional Trade Agreements (RTAs) are perceived to be trade and economic welfare instruments to deliver favourable Terms of Trade (ToT) both quantitatively and qualitatively (Bhagwati, 1991). They are also perceived as possible 'Trade Creation' (TC) instruments (Lipsey, 1957). In the last two decades, the proliferation of Regional Trade Agreements (RTAs) and the evolution of 'Factory Asia' successfully catapulted Asia into a global manufacturing hub.

India has also joined global RTAs race and promoting India as a prospective manufacturing base. India has launched seventeen multiple formats of free trade negotiations across the world out of which 13 are fully operational till 2014 (Sharma, 2016). Indo-Japan Comprehensive Economic Partnership Agreement (CEPA) is one such trade instrument to facilitate bilateral trade with Japan. In the interest of comparative perspective, we look at India's RTAs with Malaysia, South Korea and Singapore for a comprehensive understanding of how these instruments have been beneficial to India's trade related gains and how do they compare with Indo-Japan trade ToT behaviour.

ISI Model and Indo-Japan Engagement

Indo-Japan Peace Treaty of 1952 laid the basis for Indo-Japan trade, economic and technical cooperation. Japanese iron ore import from Goa in 1950s was reciprocated by extending a 18 billion Yen loan (US$50 million) to support India's second five year plan in 1958 (Takagi, 1995). This was the first-ever Japanese government-to-government yen aid loan to India (MOFA, 2011). Interestingly, during 1958 - 1965, Japan, through the World Bank Consortium, extended US$330 million loans to India which marked its highest loan amount to any developing country (Takagi, 1995). Indo-Japan Agreement on Commerce-1958 further strengthened their trade relations and provided Most Favoured Nation (MFN) status to each other in matters of taxation, tariff, enterprises and sea passage. Japan in 1980s negotiated a US $5 billion long-term loan from the IMF and in March 1991, extended US $2.45 billion loan to address India's BOP crisis (Sato, 2012).

Bilateral trade and investment continued to remain modest and political engagement cordial and cumulatively, the relationship was largely extension of cultural and civilisational orientation.

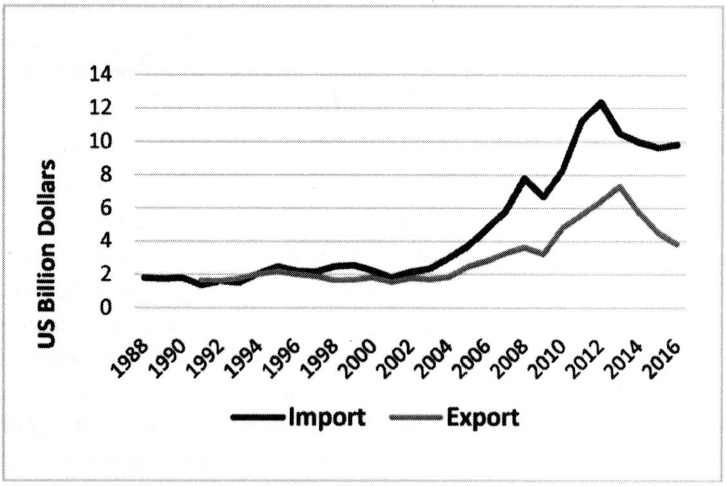

Source: https://wits.worldbank.org/

Figure 1: India's Import-Export with Japan 1988-2016.

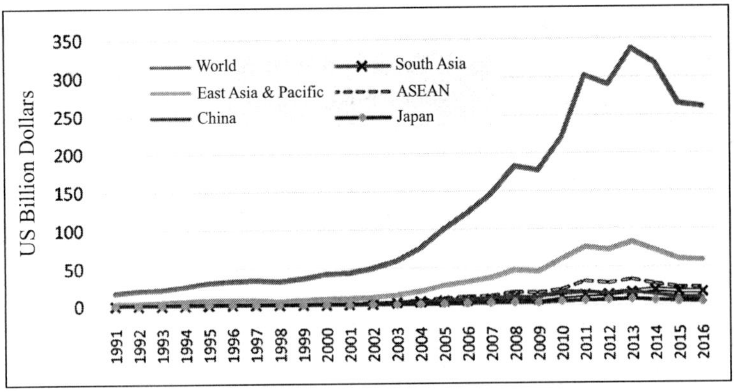

Source: https://wits.worldbank.org/

Figure 2: India's Comparative Exports 1991-2016.

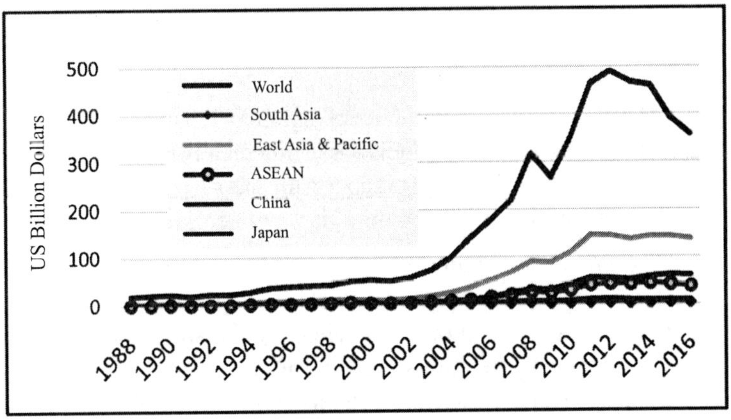

Source: https://wits.worldbank.org/

Figure 3: India's Comparative Import 1988-2016.

Post ISI Comparative Indo-Japan Trade

Throughout the Import Substitution era, Indo-Japan trade and economic relations remained rather modest. Early 1980s automobile sector collaborations and joint ventures followed with India's economic globalisation post-1991 begin to open up newer opportunity. Given India's capital and technology limitation as well as reluctant and orthodox economic reforms in the early years, economic opportunities for India continued to be far less than potential. Even today also, Indo-Japan cumulative export-import continues to be even less than US$ 20 billion only (Fig. 1). India is more import heavy is evident.

When we look at India's export behaviour since 1991 in the regional context, it is evident that nearly a fourth of India's exports are East Asia destined followed by ASEAN region. While China figures prominently as a single country, India's exports to Japan are far too negligible (Fig. 2).

On the import sector, it is again East Asia is India's primary destination followed by China. Strangely, in spite of Indo-China surcharged political climate, Indo-China bilateral trade is over US$ 68 billion today and we import over US $ 60 billion worth of goods from China. India's cumulative imports from ASEAN is far too less and hovers around US$ 38 bllion and India's imports remain even less than US$ 10 billion.

At a cursory glance, it is evident that Indo-Japan bilateral trade is rather negligible and even if India has incrementally taken an economic neoclassicism route, it is barely visible in the Indo-Japan trade behaviour. While such opinion seems obvious, it is not necessarily correct.

The fact of the matter is; the export-import absolute value is a smaller indicator to capture the depth of Indo-Japan trade and economic relations. As we look at range of economic collaborations including the rise of Japanese industries in India and increasing Indian investments in Japan, rising order of bilateral trade, aid and investment, Indo-Japan CEPA and finally the bilateral import-export *'Terms of Trade'*, it is evident that not only both countries are increasingly consolidating their economic cooperation, both seem to be at cozier economic neoclassicism order.

CEPA and India's Terms of Trade

Indo-Japan CEPA signed in 2011 was seen to be a game changer in this direction. Six years of CEPA in operation, the finer points of trade computation indeed vindicates the point through improved Terms of Trade regime which is analysed below. Given the political and strategic stress with China, Indo-Japan trade both in volume and in

Terms of Trade are expected to rise further. India also shares comparable RTAs with South Korea, Malaysia and Singapore. This paper takes comparative stock of Indo-Japan CEPA implication on ground to examine whether there is any tangible trade gain effect for India. What is evident from this comparative ToT analysis is, while Indian volume of trade is comparatively less, Indian export sector is maturing and export trade gains are beginning to be in silver lining.

Indo-Japan CEPA Provisions

1. Indo-Japan Comprehensive Economic Partnership Agreement (CEPA) has been operational since August 2011 (Embassy of Japan, 2011).
2. After a series of Joint Study Group and negotiations during 2004-11, CEPA was signed in February 2011 and came into effect in August same year (Embassy of Japan, 2011).
3. The Indio-Japan CEPA, India's third of its kind after Singapore and South Korea, covers more than 90 per cent of trade on the Indian side, a vast gamut of services, investment, IPR, customs and other trade-related issues (Embassy of Japan, 2011).
4. Only 17.4 per cent of the tariff-lines from India have been offered for immediate tariff reduction to 0 per cent.
5. Another 66.32 per cent of tariff lines shall be brought down to 0 per cent in ten years so that Indian industry has time to adjust to trade liberalisation.
6. The Japanese side offers 97 per cent of its tariff lines to 0 per cent.
7. A large number of these items are of India's export interest including seafood, agricultural products such as mangoes, citrus fruits, spices, instant tea, most spirits such as rum, whiskies, vodka etc., textile products such as woven fabrics, yarns, synthetic yarn, readymade garments, petro chemical and chemical products, cement, jewellery (GOI, 2011).
8. Indo-Japan CEPA envisages abolition of tariffs over 94 per cent of items traded between India and Japan over 10 years period. (MOFA, 2011).

India's Comparative ToT with Japan

In the context of political economy of trade, Argentine economist Raul Prebisch talked of Terms of Trade and advocated ISI model to poorer countries to protect them from adverse ToT effects while trading with developed economies (Baer, 1962). Through 1920s to 1950s, fundamental contribution on TOT by F.W. Taussig, G. S. Dorrance *et al* (Janes, 1931) go beyond mere examination of trade basket or trade volume alone. Taussig, Dorrance *et al* provided far more sophisticated tools to examine depth of trade gain as well as better computational models to measure export-import efficiency. Their contribution in measuring G-ToT (Gross Barter ToT); N-ToT (Net Barter ToT); I-ToT (Income TOT); D-ToT (Double Factorial ToT) and expanding up to Utility ToT or U-ToT intellectually and empirically helped compute ToT for finer trade gain understanding.

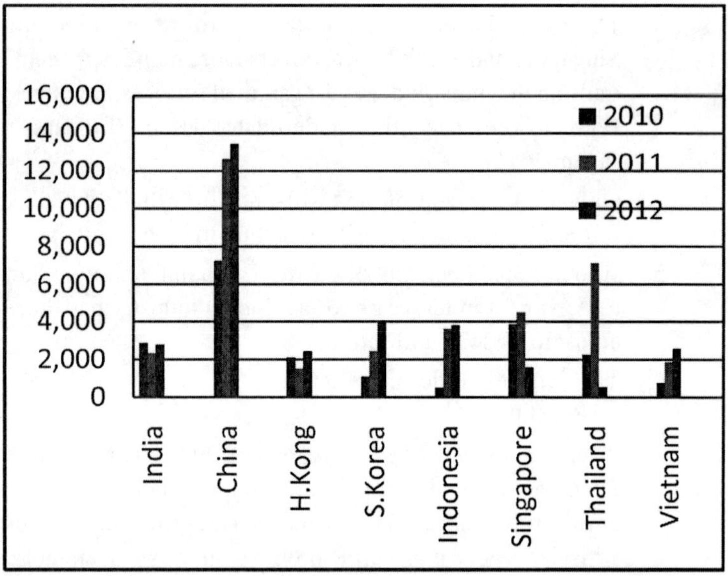

Figure 4: India's Gross Barter-ToT with Japan, Malaysia, SKorea, Singapor.

This paper analyses four stages of ToT i.e. Gross Barter Terms of Trade or G-ToT; Net or Commodity Terms of Trade or N-ToT; Income Terms of Trade or I-ToT and finally Double Factorial Terms of Trade

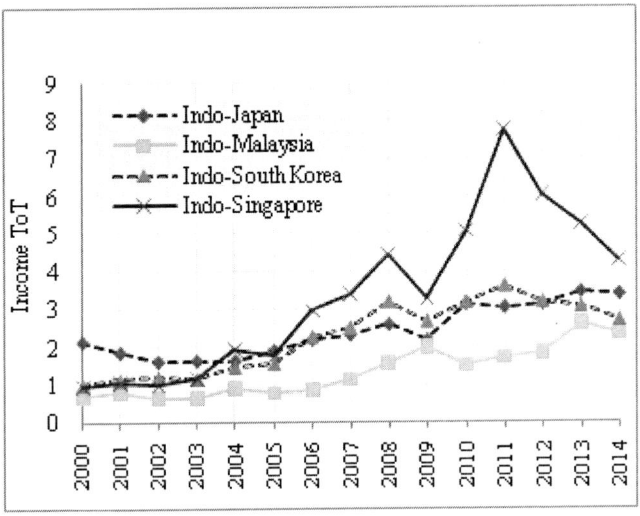

Figure 5: India's Income-ToT with Japan, Malaysia, South Korea, Singapor.

or D-ToT. Each successive ToT computation is an improvement on the previous and provides more efficient understanding of how beneficial the trade has been.

G-ToT is a simple quantitative ToT instrument to assess how one country's export and import are related quantitatively. If the country quantitatively exports more than its quantitative imports, the said country's G-ToT tends to be favourable. However, since higher quantity does not reflect trade welfare gain in a holistic manner, G-ToT tends to be a very rudimentary method of ToT calculation and very much applies to Indo-Japan trade understanding through volume of bilateral trade.

Computationally G= Mq ÷Xq ×100 where Mq is Import quantity and Xq is export quantity. Multiplication by 100 is to do away with decimal.

Commodity Terms of Trade of N-ToT however, is an improvement upon G. Using Export and Import Price Index, N shall correct limitations of G and explain how much of import can be purchased by a country in ratio to their exports. Given a favourable export price index, the country can quantitatively export less and achieve favouarable ToT too.

Computationally N[i]= Xp ÷Mp ×100 where Xp is export price index and Mp is import price index. Mp remaining stable, if Xp rises, it will create favourable ToT even if Mq is more than Xq.

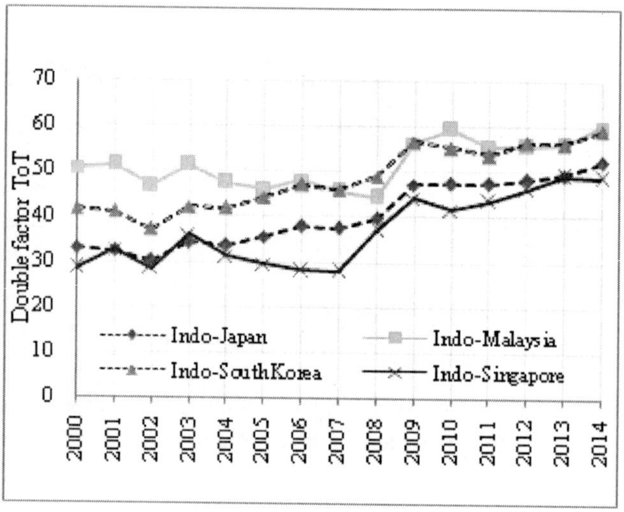

Figure 6. India's D-ToT with Japan, Malaysia, South Korea, Singapor.

Income Terms of Trade or I-ToT is a further ToT calculation improvement on the trade gain analysis and shall explain the monetised gain of a country's trade over G or N. Indian N graph available through open source has largely been negative with global countries during 2000 to 2014 except few years of periodic spurt. N remaining constant with all countries, G, I and D provide larger and finer insight to trade understanding.

Computationally I= N× Xq or N being Xp ÷Mp ×100; I = Xp ÷Mp ×100 × Xq where Xq is export quantity. Rising Xp shall create favourable ToT and along with Xp if Xq also rises, it will be a far better scenario and I-ToT of the country shall be far too good.

Further to I-ToT, there is calculation for Single Factorial ToT represented as S which is computed as NXz where in Xz is Export Productivity Ratio. This paper however, directly takes the next better computing of D-ToT where Xz and Mz (Import Productivity Ratio) are also taken to arrive at D. Calculation of S therefore is redundant.

Computationally D= N× Xz ÷Mz

Where D-ToT is computed by commodity terms of trade index multiplied by the reciprocal of the export commodity technical coefficients index, to arrive at a better resultant index providing a better guide to the ToT gain understanding than the commodity terms of trade index by itself. Since, D-ToT factors export-import productivity in trade gain analysis, it is a far better tool over G or I-ToT.

Table 1: Indo-Japan ToT

Year	*G ToT*	*I ToT*	*D ToT*	*Remark*
2000	98.90	1.867	30.301	G, I and D ToT
2014	125.09	3.365	52.252	Increasing
		Pre-CEPA ToT		
Year	*G ToT*	*I ToT*	*D ToT*	
2000	98.90	1.867	30.301	G, I and D ToT
2011	151.187	3.028	47.503	Increasing
		Post-CEPA ToT		
Year	*G ToT*	*I ToT*	*D ToT*	
2011	151.187	3.028	47.503	G Declines/I Marginal
2014	125.098	3.365	52.252	Increase/D Increases

Indo-Japan ToT Cumulative Picture

1. G-ToT increases from 98.90 in base year of 2000 to 125.09 in 2014–an increase of 1.26 times from the base year meaning India could buy more imports relative to export quantity exchanged. (See Fig. 4-6 and Table 1).
2. I-ToT increases from 1.867 in the base year to 3.365 in 2014–an increase of 1.80 times.
3. D-ToT increases from 30.301 in the base year to 52.252 in 2014- an increase of 1.74 times.

4. Overall increase of G, I and D-ToT with Japan in the entire stretch during Y 2000-2014.

Indo-Japan Pre-CEPA ToT (2000-11)

1. G-ToT increases from 98.90 in base year to 174.993 in 2009 and falls down to 144.520 in 2010 and increases to 151.187 in 2011 only marginal fall during 2000-02 and visible rise during 2008-10– a case of clear G increase (see Fig. 2-4 and Table 2).
2. I-ToT continuous rise except a marginal fall during 2000-03.
3. D-ToT marginal fall during 2001-02 and then continuous rise with visible rise in 2008-09 to plateau till 2011.

Indo-Japan Post-CEPA ToT

1. G-ToT increases from 151.187 in 2011 to 157.891 in 2012. However, from 2012 onwards G-ToT declined continuously to reach at 125.098 in 2014 i.e. the impact of CEPA on G-ToT has not been favourable - a case of relative export quantity loss (see Fig. 4-6 and Table 1). This may however be seen in the context of global economic lull.
2. I-ToT increased from 3.028 in 2011 to 3.427 in 2013 and then declined to 3.365 in 2014- a case of marginal rise i.e. case of higher trade income gain.
3. D-ToT increased from 47.503 in 2011 to 52.252 in 2014 - a clear case of D-ToT increase post CEPA execution meaning, India's export productivity (Xz) rise than Japan.
4. India seems to have achieved better export productivity (Xz) and better income gain but quantitative trade has declined (Table 2).

Rising Japan Inc. in India

While the Japanese investments for Ahmedabad-Mumbai Bullet Train project are the latest headlines in India followed by India's ambitious North Eastern States infrastructure development visions, China is Japan's primary investment destination in South Asia. Though India cannot be compared, Japan's investments in India are reasonably

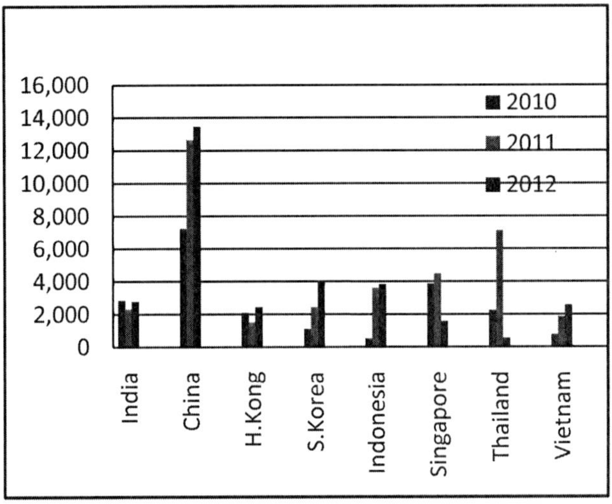

Source: JETRO 2013.

Figure 7: Japan's Comparative investment in Asian countries (U.S $ mn)

comparable with other East Asian countries and it is in rising order (Fig. 7).

The Japanese share of India's automobile market is already above 50 per cent and Japanese tier two and tier three auto component manufacturers are making inroads into India. Attractive deals in the sector are the $450 million Panasonic-Anchor buyout in April 2007 and NTT DoCoMo (Najajima, 2011). Over a five-year period, M&A and Greenfield ventures in target sectors like specialty chemicals, consumer goods, healthcare and information technology sector have registered 18 fold Japanese investments jump. Infrastructure investments in India are expected to be about a trillion US Dollars in the next five years including public private partnerships. While Japanese investment in India is continually on the rise, it is important for India to tap the Japanese investment shift from China and South East Asia which have been Japan's focus markets.

As of October, 2012, 926 Japanese corporations came into India and more than 1200 operation bases were established. Three years later in October 2015, Japanese corporations in India increased to

1229 - increase of six per cent compared to previous year (JETRO, 2016). In terms of their concentration, Maharashtra leads with 712 such establishments followed by Tamil Nadu, Karnataka, Haryana, Delhi and Punjab. However, it may be noted that almost all the provinces of India have Japanese companies/establishments which explains the depth of Japanese industrial and economic investment in India (JETRO, 2016). The establishment of Maruti-Suzuki joint venture plant in 1983 revolutionised India's automobile sector. In June 2008, Japanese pharmaceutical company Daiichi Sankyo bought a $4.6 billion controlling stake in India's largest pharmaceutical firm Ranbaxy Laboratories followed by $2.7 billion Japanese telecom giant NTT DoCoMo acquiring 26 per cent stake in Tata Teleservices Ltd. Most investments have been in automobiles, auto parts and electronics. However, some companies have invested in businesses like pharmaceuticals (EISAI), health drinks (Yakuruto), pulp (Nihon Koso) and rice processing (Yanmar). Japan's small and medium enterprises have also started to discover India as the new growth market.

On the other hand, there are few Indian companies and affiliates in Japan representing a total capital investment of Yen 1252 million (US$12.01 million). Indian MNCs are a new phenomenon post Government of India's economic liberalisation since 1991. However, as our export productivity is maturing, Indian MNCs are likely to be growing in Japan too.

Japanese Aid as Economic Diplomacy

Japanese Official Development Assistance (ODAs), Grants-in-Aid, Technical Cooperation Assistance for capacity building is a strong Indo-Japan economic engagement corridor. Japan's ODA Loans; Grant Aid and Technical Cooperation Assistance are interconnected instruments and have been early forms of Indo-Japan engagement. Japan's first ODA Loan of US$50 million in 1958 was the beginning. The ODA Loan and Japan's India-specific Country Assistance Programme has been further refined since May 2006-07 (MOFA, 2010).

Disbursed through Japan Bank for International Co-operation (JBIC), India has been the largest recipient of Japanese concessional

ODA loans since 2003-04 at annual interest rates of 0.3 per cent to 1.2 per cent with 15-30 years repayment period have greatly helped India access international capital for infrastructure projects (Nataraj, 2010). ODA funded projects like Yamuna Action Plan; 1,616 million yen Dedicated Industrial Freight Corridor Project for a 552 km-long segment; 19,832 million yen Bangalore Metro Rail Project (II); forestry, biodiversity projects in Rajasthan, Bihar National Highway Project- nearly two-third of Indian provinces have at least one such on-going projects.

Table 2: Grant Aid/Technical Cooperation from Japan to India (Million Yen)

Financial Year	*Grant Aid*	*Technical Cooperation*
2005-06	2,109	1,784
2006-07	596	2,535
2007-08	397	2,160
2008-09	428	2,451
2009-10	466	3,194
2010-11	1,159	1,681
2011-12	12	2,693
Total	**5,167**	**16,498**

Source: JICA/ Indian Embassy.

The emerging futuristic loans for India's 'Bullet Train' and North Eastern States Road and infrastructure are the rising ambitious trends. Opponents criticise Japanese loans and Yen from two counts. First this higher exposure to yen might create currency risk. Second, Japanese loans lead to high number of such contract being offered to Japan (Kundu, 2017). Given the infrastructure need in India, rising strength of Rupee and strategic connotation of Indo-Japan engagement, this could be a well placed development.

Japanese Grant Aid to India started in 1977 and the total assistance so far is 89.654 billion yen (MOFA, 2011). India has received 21,665 million Yen (Table 2) as Grant Aid and technical cooperation assistance and it is in increasing order.

Foreign Direct Investment

Japan is the fourth largest FDI investor in India (Table 3) and JBIC 2010 annual industry outlook survey indicated that 74.9 per cent of 605 Japanese companies selected India as their investment destination over the next 10 years, while 71.7 per cent chose China.

Table 3: Japanese FDI to India

Year	*Million US$*	*Per cent Change*
2001	150	-14.3
2002	146	-2.7
2003	124	-15.1
2004	139	12.1
2005	266	91.4
2006	512	92.5
2007	1506	194.1
2008	5551	268.6
2009	3664	-34.0
2010	2864	-21.8
2011	2326	-18.8
2012	2802	19.8

Source: JETRO http://www.jetro.go.jp/en/

Survey conducted since 1992 has continuously projected China as the preferred investment destination for Japanese companies. For the first time in 2010, India topped the investment destination list as most attractive location overtaking China (JBIC, 2013). The latest 2017 survey report has pushed India next to China (JBIC, 2017). Interestingly however, India fares far ahead of China in medium term future business strengthen/expand question.

Promising Sectors

Two promising sectors, the IT (Chaturvedi, 2011) and pharmaceutical sectors hold growth prospect for Indian investors in Japan. In 2012, Japan's IT / ITES market were estimated to be US$ 146 billion and pharmaceutical sector estimated to be US$ 90 billion. Only 10 per cent of Japanese IT services are outsourced/ offshored. While China shares 50 per cent market, around 70 Indian IT companies hold only one per cent market share with strong development prospects (Embassy of Japan, 2011).

Global pharmaceutical sector grows 15 per cent annually. Pharmaceutical Export Promotion Council of India (Pharmexcil), in a two-pronged strategy- 'India-Japan Pharma Alliance' or 'Brand India Pharma' in Japan, is strategizing towards Indian foothold in the US$ 90 billion Japanese market. Indian pharmaceutical majors, especially in the area of generic drugs seem to have market prospect in Japan. India's Lupin acquired Japanese Kyowa Pharmaceutical Industry and I'rom Pharmaceutical Co, in 2007 to enter the generic injectable segment and posted 14 per cent (US$143 million FY 2012-13) revenue growth in Japanese market (Balakrishnan, 2013).

On the other side, Rare Earth Elements (REE), Enhancing Sustainable Marine Resource Governance (ESMRG) in the Indian Ocean Region by collaborative Indo-Japanese Exploration and Production are seen as very promising and strategic joint development sectors which may dilute China's monopoly. China being the largest minor of rare-earth monopolises its export to China's strategic advantage which is trigger Indo-Japan collaboration in the Indian Ocean Region.

Conclusion

Japanese diplomat Sakutaro Tanino explained Tokyo - New Delhi and Tokyo–Beijing engagement ratio as 1:30 or 1:50. Examples like, 1.9 lakh Japanese visited India than over 36 lakh to China in 2012-13; only 541 Indian students study in Japan, compared to over 86,000 Chinese; there are only 7,000 Japanese residents in India, against 1.5 lakhs in China; 18,000 Indian students are learning Japanese, compared to 8.27 lakh in China; and there are 26 weekly flights between Japan and India against 668 flights between Japan and China. Tourism flows have also been dismal mainly due to the lack of cheap, clean hotel accommodation in India. These are the trends Emperor Akihito's November 2014 visit to India was trying to reverse. A similar royal visit to China in 1992 helped transform Sino-Japanese engagement quantitatively. India's Bullet Train dream is the latest symbol of Indo-

Japan engagement speed, momentum and depth which is far more rising in order in the political economy sector as well as in the strategic sector.

India and Japan at least openly do not declare their cooperation as being directed against any third country. However, the latest Malabar USA-India-Japan naval exercise and the 'Asian Quad' scripted in Manila this month is more than a declaration of China axis in India-Japan relations.

In 2007, Japanese Prime Minister, Abe Shinzo addressing Indian Parliament stressed on "confluence of the two seas." The Pacific and the Indian Oceans are "now bringing about a dynamic coupling as seas of freedom and of prosperity. A 'Broader Asia' that broke away geographical boundaries is now beginning to take on a distinct form," Japan and India "have the ability-and the responsibility–to ensure that it broadens yet further and to nurture and enrich these seas to become seas of clearest transparence (sic)." Abe' largely pitched for prosperity alliance than confrontation which India and Japan and ASEAN plus variants seem to cherish. Now Asia-Pacific maritime reimaging shifting to Indo-Pacific maritime reality, both India and Japan remain the dominant variables in the Broader Asia vision.

Economic and trade structures like ASEAN; ASEAN+3; ASEAN+6 are notions of deeper neoclassicism in Asia's economic prosperity. Since Indo-Japan collective psyche and most of the regions aspirations greatly converge with this neoclassical co-prosperity order, the future directions of the region are more likely to be market and economy centric with occasional or incremental security flash points.

Works Cited

Baer, W. (1962). The Economics of Prebisch and ECLA. *Economic Development and Cultural Change,* Vol. 10 (No. 2), pp. 169-182.

Balakrishnan, R. (2013). *Indian generic cos struggle to crack 2nd largest pharma market.* Business Standard.

Bhagwati, J. (1991). *The World Trading System at Risk.* New Jersey: Princeton University Press.

Brown, O., Shaheen, F. H. *et al,* (2005). *Regional Trade Agreements: Promoting conflict or building peace?* Ottawa: The International Institute for Sustainable Development.

Chaturvedi, A. (2011). *Loving it in Tokyo.* Business Today.

Embassy of Japan. (2011). *Japan-India Comprehensive Economic.* New Delhi: Embassy of Japan.

Embassy of Japan, N. D. (2011, February 16). *Japan-India Comprehensive Economic.* Retrieved September 1, 2016, from http://www.in.emb-japan.go.jp/Japan-India-Relations/cepa%28r%29.pdf

GOI. (2011). *commerce.nic.in/trade/ijcepa_basic_agreement.pdf.* Retrieved September 1, 2016, from http://commerce.nic.in/trade/ijcepa_basic_agreement.pdf: commerce.nic.in/trade/ijcepa_basic_agreement.pdf

Harvey, D. (2005). *A Brief History of Neoliberalism.* New York: Oxford University Press.

Hodgson, G. M. (1998). On the evolution of Thorstein Veblen's evolutionary economics. *Cambridge Journal of Economics, 22*, 415-431.

Janes, C. V. (1931). THE TERMS OF TRADE. *Economic Record, 7* (1), 64-70.

JBIC. (2017). *FY2017 Survey (the 29th) Report on Overseas Business Operations by Japanese Manufacturing Companies.* Japan Bank for International Cooperation.

JBIC. (2013). *Report on Overseas Business Operations by Japanese Manufacturing Companies.* Japan Bank for International Cooperation.

JBIC. (2013). *Report on Overseas Business Operations by Japanese Manufacturing Companies.* Japan Bank for International Cooperation.

JETRO. (2016). *Japanese Business Establishments in India.* Embassy of Japan in India, JETRO.

Kundu, T. (2017). *Is Japan's bullet train loan the best deal India has ever had?* HT Media Ltd.

Lipsey, R. G. (1957). The Theory of Customs Union:Trade Diversion and Welfare. *Economica, 24* (93), 40-46.

Masanori, K. (2012). *Japan-India Economic Relationship: Trends and prospects.* International Christian University. International Christian University.

MOFA. (2011, February 15). Retrieved from http://www.mofa.go.jp/announce/announce/2011/2/0215_01.html.

MOFA. (2010). *Country Assistance Evaluation for India:Summary.* Tokyo: Ministry of Foreign Affairs, Japan.

Najajima, H. (2011, December 8). On Japanese Firms' Interest in India. (A. Adhikari, Interviewer) New Delhi: Business Today.

Nataraj, G. (2010). *India - Japan Investment Relations: Trends and Propects.* New Delhi: Indian Council for Research on International Economic Relations.

Sato, T. (2012). *India-Japan Economic Relations: Trends and Prospects.* Kobe University: Indian Council for Research on International Economic Relations.

Sharma, A. K. (2016). *India-Singapore CECA: An Evaluation. Centre for Civil Society.* New Delhi: National Council of Applied Economic Research.

Takagi, S. (1995). From Receipt to Donor: Japan's Official Aid Flows, 1954 to 1990 and Beyond. *Essays in International Finance,* 196, 1-35.

Notes

1. The rate at which one country's goods exchange against those of another is referred to as the Terms of Trade (ToT). ToT depends on the prices of commodities entering into foreign market. Thus, ToT expresses the relation between export prices and import prices and are said to be favourable to a country when the prices of its exports are high relative to the prices of its imports. When a country's prices of imports relatively rise to its export prices, the ToT becomes unfavourable. Since N involves Export - Import Price Index which is fixed at a given year with the world trade, N for India shall remain constant with every country.

Chapter - 11

India, Japan and ASEAN: Pursuit of an 'Asian Balance'?

—*Muzaffar Hussein*

In the aftermath of Cold War, the "Rise of Asia" has become the perennial theme of narrations about global politics. The euphemistic usage of the phrase "Asian Century" is present in most intellectual prophecies about twenty-first century World Order. The prediction emphasising the importance and centrality of Asia (in domains of culture, politics and economy) is based on the emergence of rise of Asian powers: Japan, China and India on the global scene and with it the corresponding shift in the gravity of global politics and economy towards Asia. Alongside the emergence of China and Japan, the shaping up of Asian regional integration process—the ASEAN has been another exciting facet of Asian story. ASEAN launched during Cold War expanded with incorporation of other members after Cold War and has broadened the regional system through creation of various forums.

The pattern of interaction of India, Japan, ASEAN and China is central to the determination of Asian order. The recent developments in relationship between India, ASEAN and Japan is regarded as being pushed by the rise of Chinese threat and thus paving for an Asian balance (of power). Whether Asia will follow the European trajectory of balance of power involving alliance system will depend on how the relationship between India, Japan and ASEAN shapes up and their respective relationship with China. To explore this question, this chapter engages in exploration of the relationship of India and Japan with ASEAN with a focus on security and political relations. Further the chapter situates these relationships in wider context of the challenge of China.

Evolution of India's ASEAN Policy

As it stands today, India and ASEAN have extensive engagements with each other. India is involved in around 30 sectorial dialogue mechanisms, seven ministerial level interactions besides its participation in key forums of ASEAN.[1] The maturity of Indian relation with ASEAN did not occur spontaneously. It followed different trajectories based on the context of global politics. In the early years after independence, there was an impetus for pan-Asian solidarity. Both South Asia and Southeast Asia had strong association and were partners in several key global initiatives like the Conference on Asian relations, Conference on Indonesia and the Bandung Conference.[2] However, these early engagements in name of pan-Asian solidarity saw subtle quest for leadership by India and China. It was the fear of "Indian dominance" and "dominance of China" that pushed Southeast Asian participants of the Asian Relations Conference to make the early imagination of "a regional association of their own—the Southeast Asian countries minus India and China".[3]

Alongside the fear of dominance, the onset of Cold War created a defined gap between India and countries of Southeast Asia. India became inward looking and had most of its trading associations with Soviet Union. It did not participate in the Asian maritime trade—that saw the participations of Japan, South Korea, Singapore and Malaysia.[4] India viewed the very formation of ASEAN from the Cold War prism—considered it to be a creation of US to "contain Communism" in the aftermath of Vietnam War. Further, India's support for Vietnam following its invasion of Cambodia (1978) and recognition of Heng Samrin regime (1980) emerged as other major irritants in India's relation with ASEAN.[5]

The end of Cold War brought a major structural shift in the global politics: on one side Soviet Union collapsed while on the other side there was a sudden acceleration in the process of capitalist globalisation. The moment posed a major challenge for India in the form of the balance of payment crisis along with the loss of its major trading partner in Soviet. India responded by restructuring its economic policy: both domestic and international. An important aspect of this restructuring was India's rapprochement with Southeast Asia, that came in form of its "Look East Policy". Later, India reinvigorated the relationship under the frame work of "Act East".

The Look East Policy

India in 1992 under Narasimha Rao adopted its 'Look East' policy with objectives to pursue stronger economic and cultural relations with the nations of Asia-Pacific region. With the objective to reduce their independence on Japan, China and West, the ASEAN countries gave a positive response to Indian overtures. India was accepted as Sectoral Dialogue partner of ASEAN in 1992, full Dialogue partner in 1996 and became the member of Asian Regional Forum (ARF) and began participating in ASEAN Post-Ministerial Conferences in 1996.[6]

A brief halt came in the linear progression of India's Look East Policy following Asian Financial Crisis of 1998 and India's nuclear tests.[7] However, they did not emerge as major road blocks and the process resumed. The tempered reaction of ASEAN towards India's nuclear tests can be explained in terms of its own "concerns over China's rise and dominant role in Southeast Asia".[8] The Look East Policy further evolved under Prime Minister Atal Bihari Vajpayee. Vajpayee pursued an extensive engagement with the new ASEN countries like Cambodia, Laos, Myanmar and Vietnam (CLMV countries). Here India pushed for the "Mekong-Ganges Rivers Cooperation Project for promotion of tourism culture and education. The project involved Cambodia, Myanmar, Laos, Vietnam, Thailand and Philippines. The new millennium took Indian engagement with ASEAN further ahead. The development of Summit level-partnership between India and ASEAN is often described as the beginning of phase two of the Look East Policy. At the Bali Summit (2003), India concluded three key agreements with ASEAN: Framework Agreement on Comprehensive Security, Joint Declaration on Cooperation in Combatting International Terrorism, and India's accession to ASEAN's Treaty of Amity and Cooperation. With these, India gradually moved beyond the economic to "security and political levels" in its engagements with ASEAN.[9] Many argued that the shift was partially dictated by the China factor. However, in the aftermath of the beginning of phase two of the relationship, India pursued cooperative engagements with China, thus asserting the "phase two (of Look East) is not driven by a fear of China."[10]

India's move from economic to security and political gradually progressed since the beginning of phase two of Look East policy. India was admitted as founding member of the East Asia Summit (EAS). EAS marked the formal inclusion of non-ASEAN countries: Japan, China, South Korea, India, Australia, and New Zealand in the regional architecture of Southeast Asia. Due to the presence of other members, it is also regarded as ASEAN+6.[11] Singapore, Indonesia and Thailand pushed for India's inclusion in the Summit. Indian presence is regarded to have been ensured "to play a counter-weight role vis-à-vis China".[12] This was followed by ASEAN Defence Ministers' Meeting Plus (ADMM-Plus) in 2010 and ASEAN Maritime Security Forum (EAMSF) of 2012.[13] On ASEAN's part, admission of India to the key institutions of the region's architecture is a own strategy to dilute both the influence of China as well as that of extra-regional great powers as US and thus preserve its own economic and strategic autonomy.[14] Institutionalising a regular security engagement, India and ASEAN established the Delhi Dialogue (a premier annual track 1.5 event) in 2009. It has emerged as an important stock taking exercise of global developments—particularly with potential security implications.[15] Overall, "Look East" Policy had economy as its central issue area. There was a gradual inclusion of security and political matters in India-ASEAN relationship. This expansion also corresponded with the Southeast Asian countries engagements with each other under the ambit of ASEAN. Their initiative of regional trade agreements has gradually expanded to range of issues: security, culture, energy and environment.[16]

'Act East': Reconfiguration of Indian Eastward Policy

The change in leadership in New Delhi brought a change in its approach towards ASEAN. Prime Minister Narendra Modi reframed Look East Policy as 'Act East Policy' in November 2014 at the

Twelfth ASEAN India Summit. The shift was needed as Foreign Minister Sushma Swaraj claimed because "[L]ook East is no longer adequate; now we need Act East policy" (Manish Chand).[17] The replacement of 'Look' with 'Act' entailed a shift to an "action-oriented approach" towards ASEAN with a greater priority to "security" along with connectivity and regional integration.[18] As officially stated, an important objective of Act East Policy is to "develop strategic relationship with countries in the Asia-Pacific region through continuous engagement at bilateral, regional and multilateral levels". Strategic engagement thus became central to India's outlook towards Asia-Pacific and with it, India upgraded its "relations to strategic partnership" with Japan, Australia and South Korea along with ASEAN nations.[19] Act East not only made a proactive push towards security, but brought within the framework of policy actors beyond ASEAN. Despite the broadening of the ambit (in terms of actors), India considers ASEAN as pivot to its Act East Policy.[20]

Strategically, Act East seeks to expand India's role in the regional maritime order. In that direction, India has expanded its naval presence in South China Sea. It has also imparted submarine training to Vietnamese and has pursued a proposal to impart similar training to Indonesia.[21] India and Vietnam pushed for a "communique" in 2014—opposing "threats to freedom of navigation and use of coercion in the South China Sea". In engaging with management of maritime affairs, India has emphasised the role of International Law and other norms in governance of maritime order. Indian approach has found a due support from US—which identifies its own interest in preservation of international legal frameworks related with sea. The signing of defence framework by India and US, that commits to increase their respective capability to secure "freedom of navigation across sea lanes of communication" was an indication of this convergence.[22]

Overall, from "Look East" to "Act East", India has been successful in first making its economic presence in Asia-Pacific/Indo-Pacific and later expanding that to security and strategic domain. In moving towards strategic direction, India has found a convergence with Japan and US in their consensus over centrality of legal and normative framework in the management and governance of maritime affairs.

India's engagement has often been interpreted as an exercise to balance China. However, India has been simultaneously engaging with China and been prompt in refuting the claim of its engagements in Southeast Asia being directed towards China.

Trajectory of Japan-ASEAN Relationship

In the aftermath of World War II, Japan's policy and engagements have been oriented towards US and West. It's engagements in Asia were dictated by the coupling of its relationship with US. However, during the Cold War and its aftermath Japanese engagement with Southeast Asia evolved from a weak economic engagement to proactive security initiatives. The end of Cold War and the rise of China presented the contextual framework within which Japan engaged with Southeast Asia in past two decades.

The Cold War Era Engagements

Much of Japan's policy towards Southeast Asian countries during the Cold War period was driven by Japan's own association with US and the corresponding affiliation with West—in its wider struggle with Communism. Japan's post-war engagement in Southeast Asia revolved around war reparations and economic assistance. Japan offered substantial Official Development Assistance (ODA) to countries of Southeast Asia for purpose of nation building. The framework for Japan's engagement in Asia was defined by US-Japan Mutual Security Treaty and Yoshida doctrine (laid by Japanese Prime Minister Yoshida Shigeru) defined the grand strategy for post-war Japan. Both of collectively emphasised economy as the main domain of Japanese policy (domestic and international) and recognised US security role for Japan.[23] US strategic presence in East Asia in post-war era was a natural outcome of these arrangements. During this phase, Japan actively pursued its economic interest in Southeast Asia. Southeast Asia was a key supplier of raw materials and had the potential to be the market for its products.[24] Japan responded positively to the declaration of formation of ASEAN by when the five Southeast Asian countries: Thailand, Singapore, Philippines, Malaysia and Indonesia. Japan displayed a keen support to the Asian regional integration process. However, the relationship between ASEAN and Japan turned cold owing to ASEAN's adoption of Malaysian proposal of Zone of Peace, Freedom and Neutrality in 1971. Owing to its own partnership with US, Japan was averse to the idea/position of neutrality. Further, a perception started growing that Japan's economic engagements—through aid and investments are designed to control Southeast Asian states by ensuring economic dependence on Japan. This distrust found an expression in form of the anti-Japanese movement—the Tanaka riots that spread throughout Southeast Asia.[25]

The relationship began improving with ASEAN-Japan Summit (1977). At the second summit meeting, the then Japanese Prime Minister Takeo Fukuda announced his "Fukuda Doctrine"—laying out the framework for ASEAN-Japan relations.[26] The framework was based on three pillars: rejection of role of military power, building of relationship of mutual confidence based on "heart-to-heart" understanding and cooperation from perspective of an equal partner. Fukuda doctrine sought to address the perception of Japan's economic dominance in Southeast Asia.[27] The emphasis on "equality" was a corrective measure. The Fukuda doctrine also came in the context of US withdrawal from Vietnam in 1976. Through it, Japan sought to adopt a more independent foreign policy—a departure from its earlier Western-oriented stance influenced by its strong association with US.[28] Japan displayed international activism in the aftermath of Vietnam's invasion of Cambodia in 1978. Cambodian issue that lasted till 1991 became the defining framework not only in Japan-ASEAN's relation but also ASEAN own functioning. In exercising its political role, Japan adopted "Support ASEAN" policy and established and synergy with ASEAN in the pursuit of regional stability and peace.[29]

Post-Cold War Engagements

The end of Cold War shifted the framework of operation of international politics from global to regional level. Regionalism, regional security and economic arrangements became the trend both in Asia and rest of the world. In case of ASEAN, the resolution of Cambodian issue meant that the whole energy now can be devoted to regional integration. In the geopolitical landscape, the aftermath of Cold War saw the rise of China. China rose to dominate both economic and political landscape. These developments corresponded with the declining Japanese influence.

The Hashimito Doctrine (1997), propounded by Japan's PM Ryutaro Hashimoto was response to this changed geopolitical landscape. The doctrine called for broadening and deepening of exchanges between Japan and ASEAN, expansion of cultural cooperation and coordinated efforts by both to tackle problems of international community. However, the momentum went down with the onset of Asian financial crisis. Japan initially intervened with aid for emergency financial assistance. Later, under Obuchi plan (propounded by then Japanese PM Keizo Obuchi), Japan shifted the focus of aid from emergency assistance to long-term recovery of Southeast Asian economies.[30]

After the financial crisis, ASEAN recognised the significance of economic integration and need to develop partnerships with the big actors in East Asia. From this recognition emerged the Chiang Mai Initiative—multilateral currency swap arrangement and the ASEAN +3 (Japan, South Korea and China).[31] Subsequently, ASEAN proposed East Asian Summit and Japan became part of it. The proactive engagement which Japan began with Hashimato doctrine was pushed further through its pursuits Miyazawa plan, the Japan-ASEAN summit meeting and consolidations of strategic partnership with ASEAN under Prime Minister Shinzo Abe.[32]

Over the course of last two decades, ASEAN has been pursuing a uniform yardstick towards different countries in its approach towards issues of security and peace. It has sought to ensure multilateralism and participation of all the important actors. Alongside it pursuits of free trade agreements, ASEAN has also sought collaborations of actors from outside the region within the ambit of Treaty of Amity and Cooperation in Southeast Asia (TAC), which entails "respect for sovereignty, peaceful resolutions of disputes, and cooperation to stabilise order in the region". Japan along with other the important powers of the Asia Pacific region (China, India, South Korea and Australia) have acceded to the treaty. Alongside, there has been marked development in Japan's own political and security relations with ASEAN outside these multi-actor frameworks. The Joint Declaration for Enhancing ASEAN-Japan Strategic Partnership for Prospering Together (the Bali Declaration) of 2011 recognises "political-security" as an important strategy for strengthening of ASEAN-Japan partnership.[33]

A proactive shift in domain of Japan's security and strategy cooperation with ASEAN came after the return of Prime Minister Shinzo Abe to his office in December 2012. In the very first year, Abe visited all the ten countries of ASEAN. The shift was further facilitated by the change in Japan's domestic defence policy—that came with an end to the ban on arms exports in 2014. This opened the scope for defence "equipment and technology cooperation and transfers". Subsequently, there has been a surge in defence related interactions.[34] Japan has also its course of security engagements in future through the "Vientiane Vision" unveiled by Japanese Defence Minister Tomomi Inada. Under the vision, Japan would pursue defence cooperation with ASEAN states for the objective of promotion of rule of law and strengthening of maritime security. Cooperation, support and assistance are defined as the action mechanisms under the vision.[35]

Overall, from the end of Cold War to the promulgation of Vientiane vision, Japan has gradually shifted from economic to security and strategic domain. In the process Japan is transforming itself into a key player in the domain of security in the Asia-Pacific Region.

Striking the 'Balance'

The trajectory relationship of ASEAN with both India and Japan reveals that there has been a gradual but robust addition of security and strategic matters to the framework of their relationships. For all of them, these transitions have come at the backdrop of rising China in general and Chinese assertiveness in recent past in the maritime domain—the East China Sea and South China Sea. China from late 1990s to late 2000 pursued an approach of coexistence in management of maritime affairs. However, since March 2009, when patrol vessel, it shifted to a more hard-line approach toward maritime issues. For Japan, the relation with China in the maritime domain became tense over Senkaku Islands. Likewise, for other ASEAN countries, there has been a growing Chinese assertiveness on territorial issues and the issues of Spratly Islands and the Scarborough Reef.[36] In case of India, tension with China has emerged in a wider context involving both the maritime management in Asia-Pacific and engagements with China at bilateral level.

The developments in security and strategic engagements of Indian and Japan have come alongside developments in their relationship at bilateral level and other forums. At the bilateral level, India and Japan signed security agreement to advance "security cooperation" in 2008 in range of areas such as "sea-lane safety and defence collaboration to disaster management and counterterrorism". India-Japan Security arrangement came after the 2007 Japan-Australia accord. In terms of commonality, both agreements emphasised commitment to norms and values as democracy, freedom, human rights and rule of law. They talked of defence cooperation not only at bilateral level, but also in the context of "security in the Asia-Pacific".[37] An important question that guides the engagement is the need to respond to growing Chinese influence—evident in its ambitious projects like Belt and Road Initiative—pushing for development of massive infrastructure to increase both land and sea trade across Asia and beyond. Prime Minister Shinzo Abe and his Indian counterpart in their meeting in September 2017 have emphasised the role and importance of all countries (not just China) in development and use of "connectivity infrastructure in an open, transparent and non-exclusive manner".[38] More specifically, in the maritime order, both Japan and India have asserted their commitment to freedom of navigation and rule-based regime.[39]

Japan's own active involvement in security activism has also grown largely due to US desire to see Japan stepping in as a player in Asian order. This is also outcome of a shift in foreign policy approach within US, where it seeks to put some responsibilities on "strong regional allies and partners". In such context of policy shift, Japan (along with India) fits the bill as US's partner in management of order in East Asia.[40] The recent revival of 'quad'—a naval umbrella involving India, Japan, Australia along with US can be regarded to be directed at management of Asia with the US and with China (excluded from the group) being implicitly identified as the main challenge in management of Asian maritime order. However, the group is still in inception—stage with key tasks still undefined. Though the Quad formation came in the backdrop of growing Chinese aggression, the grouping did not produce any statement directed at China. They only presented their vision for "prosperity and security in a free and open Indo-Pacific region".[41] US since 2005 has been trying to rope in India into the network of "valued based relationship" that surrounds China. While India has been reluctant to be part of any security alliance/ arrangement being solely directed at China. Even the Quad agreement formed at the sidelines of ARF was projected more as being linked with ASEAN, thus bringing it more in the framework of the governance institution than security alliance in the classic sense of balance of power.[42]

Conclusion: A Future of Partnerships

The two decades after the end of the Cold War has witnessed China, ASEAN and India join Japan big actors of global economy. The appearance of these actors on global scene and their continuing growth has brought back Asia at the centre stage of global politics—with India, Japan and ASEAN emerging as important actors. In their engagement with maritime order in Asia-Pacific, India, Japan and ASEAN has seen a convergence in their priority—of a regime and law based maritime order. These convergences have allowed them to come together and build partnerships. In this quest, China has emerged as a common concern. However, these arrangements are nowhere near an "alliance system"—leading to a classic balance of power.

With respect to China, both India and Japan along with ASEAN are involved in extensive trade interactions. Further, despite its arm twisting China on its own also has called for engagements and partnerships. China has also displayed willingness to be part of regime-based interactions. This was particularly evident in the way it pushed for free-trade deal with ASEAN and willingness to be part of multilateral associations creating one of its own, the East Asian Summit, which pointedly excludes the United States".[43] Further, China in itself does not favours an emergence of any balance against itself. It was interesting to see Chinese criticism to the response as articulated by its Foreign Ministry spokesperson Geng Shuang. China rather than criticising it's the formation was more annoyed with its exclusion and wanted it to be "open and inclusive" leading to a win-win cooperation and thus would prevent politicisation of the matter.[44]

On its part, India also has thoroughly asserted its strategic autonomy and has refuted the membership of "contain China effort". It has rather pursued "Engagement with China" as the priority.[45] Even after the recent "Quad" formation, India has not stopped engagements at other forums. India has pushed for meeting with China under the framework of Russia, India, China (RIC) meet to push to discuss the "deepening of coordination in Asia Pacific region".[46] Overall, India has pursued a distinct approach of engagements with multiple actors at multiple levels. Rather than having entire focus on singular country, India has pursued a "widened defence contacts" and in the process, has engaged in a "multi-directional defence diplomacy in Asia".[47]

The emerging Asian order is being driven by a system of function based frameworks which are both bilateral and multilateral. Further, an emphasis on non-traditional security issues like Terrorism has allowed easier coordination without generating corresponding suspicion. The last couple of decades have witnessed occasions of Chinese assertions, however in over all matrix of Asian security, 'balance' has been ensured by a web of multi-level processes involving different actors.

Notes

1. Suyash Desai, "Revisiting India ASEAN Relations", *The Diplomat*, 18 Nov. 2017, https://thediplomat.com/2017/11/revisiting-asean-india-relations/.
2. Amitav Acharya, "The Idea of Asia", *Asia Policy*, no.9, (January 2010), pp. 32-39; Lavina Lee, "India as a Nation of Consequence in Asia: the Potential and Limitations of India's 'Act East' Policy", *The Journal of East Asian Affairs*, Vol. 29 No. 2 (Winter 2015), pp. 67-104.
3. Acharya, pp. 36-37.
4. Lavina Lee (2015), pp. 71.
5. Chietigj Bajpaee, "Deciphering India's Look East/Act East Policy", *Contemporary Southeast Asia: A Journal of International and Strategic Affairs,* Vol. 39, No. 2 (August 2017), pp. 348-372; Suyash Desai, (2017).
6. Zhao Hong, "India and China: Rivals or Partners in Southeast Asia", *Contemporary South East* Asia, Vol. 29, No. 1 (April 2007), pp. 121-142; Suyash Desai, (2017); Harsh V. Pant and Avantika Deb, "India-ASEAN

Partnership at 25", http://www.orfonline.org/research/india-asean-partnership-at-25/.

7. Chietigj Bajpaee (2017), p. 350.
8. Zhao Hong (2007), pp. 123-124.
9. Chietigj Bajpaee (2017), p. 352.
10. C. Raja Mohan, "Look East Policy: Phase Two", *The Hindu*, 9 Oct. 2003, http://www.thehindu.com/2003/10/09/stories/2003100901571000.htm.
11. Mohit Anand, "India-ASEAN Relations: Analysing Regional Implications", IPCS Special Report, May 2009.
12. Zhao Hong (2007), p. 124.
13. Chietigj Bajpaee (2017), p. 356.
14. Laving Lee (2015), pp. 79-80.
15. MEA, "India-ASEAN Relations", Ministry of External Affairs, http://mea.gov.in/Portal/ForeignRelation/India-ASEAN_Relations.pdf.
16. SD Muni. 2006. "East Asia Summit and India," Institute of South Asian Studies Working Paper, No. 13.
17. Quoted in Manish Chand, "Act Asia: India's ASEAN Journey", Ministry of External Affairs, 10, Nov. 2010, www.mea.gov.in/in-focus-article.htm?24216/Act+East+Indias+ASEAN+Journey.
18. Manish Chand, (2014).
19. Ministry of External Affairs (MEA), "Question No.4062. Act East Policy", 23 Dec 2015, http://www.mea.gov.in/lok-sabha.htm?dtl/26237/QUESTION_NO4062_ACT_EAST_POLICY.
20. Manish Chand, (2014).
21. Tang Ming Hui and Nazia Hussain, "Japan and India: Concerted Efforts at Regional Diplomacy", *The Diplomat*, 10, April 2017, https://thediplomat.com/2017/04/japan-and-india-concerted-efforts-at-regional-diplomacy/.
22. Indian Express, "India's Act East Policy balancing China in the Region: Think Tank", *Indian Express,* 24 July, 2015, indianexpress.com/article/india/india-others/indias-act-east-policy-balancing-china-in-the-region-thinktank/
23. Beina Xu, "US-Japan Security Alliance", *Council on Foreign Relations,* 1 July 2014, https://www.cfr.org/backgrounder/us-japan-security-alliance
24. Yeo Lay Hwee, "Japan, ASEAN and the Construction of an East Asian Community", *Contemporary Southeast Asia: A Journal of International and Strategic Affairs,* Vol. 28, No. 2, (August 2006), pp. 259-275.
25. Sueo Sudo, *Evolution of ASEAN-Japan Relations*, (Singapore: ISEAS, 2005); Bhubhindar Singh, "ASEAN's Perceptions of Japan: Change and Continuity", *Asian Survey*, Vol. 42, No. 2 (March/April 2002), pp. 276-296.

26. Business Times, "ASEAN-JAPAN Relations: Past and Present", 26 April, 2017, http://www.businesstimes.com.sg/hub/asean-japan-special/asean-japan-relations-past-and-present.
27. Oba Mie, "Challenges to the New ASEAN-Japan Partnership in the Changing Circumstances", *Japan Policy Forum,* 26 March, 2014, URL: http://www.japanpolicyforum.jp/archives/diplomacy/pt20140326014352.html.
28. S. Jawed Masood, "Japanese Foreign Policy and Regionalism", in S. Jawed Masood (eds.) *Japan and East Asian Regionalism*, (New York: Routledge, 2001).
29. Peng Er. Lam, "Japan's Diplomatic Initiatives in Southeast Asia", in S. Jawed Masood (eds.) *Japan and East Asian Regionalism*, (New York: Routledge, 2001); Yeo Lay Hwee (2006), pp. 260.
30. Bhubhindar Singh, "ASEAN's Perceptions of Japan: Change and Continuity", *Asian Survey*, Vol. 42. No. 2. (March/April 2002), pp. 276-296.
31. Chietigj Bajpaee, " a", pp. 356.
32. Sueo Sudo, "Japan's ASEAN Policy: Reactive or Proactive in the Face of a Rising China in East Asia?", *Asian Perspective*, Vol. 33, No. 1, pp. 137-158.
33. Oba Mie, (2014).
34. Prashanth Parameswaran, "Japan Reveals First ASEAN Defense Initiative with Vientiane Vision", *The Diplomat,* 26, Nov. 2016, https://thediplomat.com/2016/11/japan-reveals-first-asean-defense-initiative-with-vientiane-vision/.
35. Prashanth Parameswaran, "Japan Reveals First ASEAN Defense Initiative with Vientiane Vision".
36. Oba Mie, (2014).
37. Brahma Chellaney, "Different playbooks aimed at balanching Asia's powers", *The Japan Times*, 3, Nov. 2008, https://www.japantimes.co.jp/opinion/2008/11/03/commentary/different-playbooks-aimed-at-balancing-asias-powers/#.WigV90xuJOw.
38. Hiroyuki Akita, "ASEAN Seeks Strong Japanese Presence in Asia to Counter China", *Nikkei Asian Review,* 19 September 2017, https://asia.nikkei.com/Politics-Economy/International-Relations/ASEAN-seeks-strong-Japanese-presence-in-Asia-to-counter-China.
39. Tang Ming Hui and Nazia Hussain, "Japan and India: Concerted Efforts at Regional Diplomacy", *The Diplomat*, 10, April 2017, https://thediplomat.com/2017/04/japan-and-india-concerted-efforts-at-regional-diplomacy/.
40. http://www.dw.com/en/japan-asean-ties-may-stabilize-balance-of-power/a-17673423.
41. Maha Siddiqui, "India Looks to Balance Regional Equations with China After Quad Talks", *CNN-NEWS 18,* 6 Dec. 2017, http://www.news18.com/

news/india/india-looks-to-balance-regional-equations-with-china-after-quad-talks-1596967.html.

42. Siddartha Vardarajan, "Four-power meeting drew Chinese de'marche", *The Hindu,* 14 June 2017,https://svaradarajan.com/2007/06/14/four-power-meeting-drew-chinese-demarche/.
43. Fareed Zakaria, *The Post-American World and the Rise of the Rest,* (Gurgaon: Penguin, 2008), pp. 119-120.
44. "India, US, Japan and Australia must not target us: China", *Economic Times,* 13 Nov. 2017, https://economictimes.indiatimes.com/news/defence/india-us-japan-and-australia-must-not-target-us-china/articleshow/61628031.cms.
45. The Hindu, "PM: India not part of "contain China" effort", *The Hindu,* 11 Jan. 2008, http://www.thehindu.com/todays-paper/tp-national/PM-India-not-part-of-ldquocontain-Chinardquo-effort/article15141882.ece.
46. Elizabteh Roche, "RIC meet: Foreign ministers of Russia, India, China meet today to boost Asia-Pacific relations", *Livemint*, 11 Dec. 2017, www.livemint.com/Politics/i3GWpbkjjX4QL2snEEbAIL/RIC-meet-Foreign-ministers-of-Russia-India-China-meet-tod.html.
47. C Raja Mohan, (2003).

Chapter - 12

From Cordiality to Estrangement to Maturity: An Analysis of India-Japan Relations

—Reyaz Ahmad Ganaie

Long before Donald Trump was elected as the President of the United States, a remaking of the world order was set in motion with the unfolding of the US-led 'War on Terror'. George W. Bush's and Barack Obama's War on Terror campaign resulted in draining America's power (in terms of men, material, and moral authority) to the extent that the United States steadily began to manifest a discernible decline in terms of the undisputed hegemonic position it had acquired as a result of the disintegration of the erstwhile USSR. The primacy and leadership that the United States assumed with the onset of the post-Cold War era is now beginning to show unmistakable fractures. It won't be an exaggeration to say that the 'unipolar world' characterisation of the world order is no longer relevant, and that a fast-emerging multi-polar world is bound to become the norm in the near future. While there are Western competitors to the United States including most notably Germany, Canada, France and Britain; it is the Asian theatre that possesses enormous potential to tilt the global balance of power equation in its favour. In Asia, this tilt can be brought about by the rising economic profile of ASEAN nations or, in isolation, by an emerging India, Japan and most importantly, China.

There is little disagreement over the issue as to which country could possibly fill the vacuum that the decline of the United States would create at the international level. With its robust economy at home and an ever increasing trade and investment presence abroad, China has long been manifesting its dominance not just in Asia but has also started to flex muscles elsewhere as well. The irony of contemporary international politics is that the United States, under the leadership of President Trump, appears to be gearing for adopting an 'isolationist' mode in order to revamp and revitalise US economy. Trump's 'America First' and his regular jibes and tirades against China, Mexico, India and other major US trading partners clearly demonstrates a rather discomforting trend in US foreign policy: that the liberal order which became the bedrock of US preponderance–both in terms of its economic prowess and in terms of assuming the role of a watchdog for promotion of individual freedom, democracy and human rights–is now left without its most ardent advocate. Quite ironically, it is China–a state ruled by a communist party–which now appears to be shouldering the responsibility of protecting the same liberal order.

It is against the backdrop of a rising China–a country with which both New Delhi and Tokyo don't enjoy friendly ties–that India-Japan relations becomes all the more important, for, if nurtured properly, it has the potential to become a game-changer as far as the strategic landscape in Indo-Pacific region is concerned. Therefore, the recent high profile visits made by Indian Prime Minister Narendra Modi and his Japanese counterpart Shinzo Abe are a step towards the translation of that potential into a reality thereby setting in motion the development of, as Professor Swaran Singh calls it, the 'defining partnership' of twenty-first century.[1]

India-Japan Relations: A Historical Background

While India was preparing for freedom, India's Prime Minister Jawaharlal Nehru (Head of the Provisional Government at the time) began to assert that India's new status endowed it with the 'leadership' of Asia. Towards this end, under Nehru's command, Delhi hosted the Asian Relations Conference of March-April 1947, which *inter alia* was to act as the platform for fostering unity among the nations of Asia and to express solidarity with those nations which were yet to achieve independence from the yoke of European colonialism. Nehru's 'leadership of Asia' project was voiced unequivocally at the 1949

Conference on Indonesia in Delhi and the 1955 Bandung Conference in which India proclaimed itself to be the leader of Asia's march towards independence.[2] However, as soon as India got embroiled in Cold War politics, and, as a result, lost its image of being a purely non-aligned country, India's 'leadership' project lost its moral vigour. In fact, Indian foreign policy witnessed an overt tilt in favour of West Asia as a result of Delhi's concerns for energy security. To add to India's declining interest in fostering better relations with the nations to its East was the ever present rivalry and territorial disputes with China and Pakistan warranting priority over all other foreign policy issues.

A remarkable shift in India's foreign policy took place as a result of both the end of Cold War and India restructuring its economy in conformity with the paradigm of liberalisation. These two changes forced India to 'Look East' and to revive its relations with the fast emerging economies in East Asia. India's economic reforms of 1991 compelled New Delhi to seek new trading partners in order to compete in an entirely new economic environment which it had not yet taken part in, structural adjustments in economy necessitated a reconfiguring of India's foreign policy outlook. This eventually paved the way for India's 'Look East Policy', launched by Indian Prime Minister P.V. Narasimha Rao in 1992. Initially, Look East Policy focussed on engagement with ASEAN countries only; later, its ambit was widened so as to include all nations East of India while retaining ASEAN as the core. In 2003, Yashwant Sinha, the then External Affairs Minister of India, while elaborating on the expanded meaning of 'East' in India's Look East Policy remarked:

> *The first phase of India's Look East Policy was ASEAN-centred and focussed primarily on trade and investment linkages. The new phase of this policy is characterised by an expanded definition of 'East', extending from Australia to East Asia, with ASEAN as its core. The new phase also marks a shift from trade to wider economic and security issues, including joint efforts to protect the sea-lanes and coordinate counter-terrorism activities.*[3]

The expansion in the ambit of Look East Policy implied an interest on part of New Delhi not only to build economic ties but to consolidate strategic partnerships with these countries in order to create for itself a distinct power position in Asia that would in turn help India in consolidating its power profile at the global level. This is the broad framework within which India-Japan relations need to be situated if one is to look at the changing dynamics and fortunes of New Delhi-Tokyo ties.

The genesis of India-Japan relations long predates their emergence as modern nation states. Some historical accounts trace the beginning of this relationship to sixth century A.D. during the reign of Emperor Kimmei (539-571 A.D.).[4] In its formative phase, India-Japan relations was anchored and driven by the shared spiritual and cultural bond of Buddhism. This bond became stronger when Buddhism was adopted as a state religion in Japan under the rule of Prince Umayado (593-622 A.D.).[5] This paved the way for Japanese to travel to India in order to pursue their spiritual yearning and also acted as a catalyst for the Buddhist preachers in India to travel to Japan to further the cause of their religion. Spiritual linkage, with the passage of time, produced a spill over effect in so far as it facilitated the development of economic relations between the two countries. In fact, owing to fast-growing spinning industry in Japan, India became a chief source of importing raw cotton. Further, India also provided a profitable market for Japanese goods.

This early cordiality later on encompassed the 'political' element as well when, during India's national freedom struggle, Japan became a 'second home' to many of India's prominent nationalist leaders like Subash Chandra Bose, Maulavi Barkatulla, Rash Bihari Bose and Bhagat Singh. Some scholars, however, opine that the support provided by Japan was driven by an ulterior motive which by the time had itself become an imperial power. They argue that Japanese support for India's freedom struggle was actually a ploy to get rid of British presence in the subcontinent so that Japan itself could invade India.[6] This was not to happen since Japan got embroiled in an unprecedented conflict with the United States when the former launched a miscalculated pre-emptive military strike on Pearl Harbour naval base on 7 December 1941 forcing United States out of the 'isolationist shell' and prompting Washington to avenge the attack by using nuclear weapons against Japanese cities of Hiroshima and Nagasaki. The devastation caused by the twin atomic bombs forced Japan to surrender unconditionally thereby decimating Tokyo's imperial designs. Japan's imperial adventurism, prior to and during the Second World War, had caused India-Japan relations to deteriorate. The end of Second World War, however, infused a new life in Indo-Japan relations and ended the estrangement caused earlier. India, under Prime Minister Nehru, was keen to bring Japan under the umbrella of non-alignment, for he feared Japan's alliance either with the United States or Soviet Union would breed Cold War rivalry among the nations of Asia. Even though Japan did not join NAM, yet India-Japan relations gained some much needed momentum when the two countries signed India-Japan Peace Treaty in June 1952. The treaty was concluded with the aim of improving bilateral ties, maintaining peace and exploring avenues for greater economic and commercial linkages. The treaty declared that "there shall be firm and perpetual peace and amity between India and Japan and their peoples."[7] The treaty, simply put, was an effort to resurrect a historical relationship in tune with the realities of the twentieth century.

The enthusiasm associated with the signing of the Peace Treaty, however, did not last long as Cold War politics cast its shadow on India-Japan relations with the two countries finding themselves on the opposite sides of international political landscape. Having remained under US influence since the end of Second World War, Japan became an important American ally in the Asia-Pacific region. India, on the other hand, exhibited a distinctive tilt in favour of USSR with little regard for New Delhi's avowed commitment to Non-Alignment Movement. This divergence during the Cold War era became a cause for the loss of momentum in taking forward the cordiality in their bilateral relations. To add to this divergence in foreign policy outlook was India's decision to conduct nuclear tests in 1974. Japan's reaction to the tests was one of utter shock as Tokyo suspended Official Development Assistance (ODA)[8] to India with immediate effect. Moreover, Japan also 'opposed financial support for India from the multilateral institutions in which it had a say.'[9] In fact, Tokyo took a firm stand that unless India signed Comprehensive Test Ban Treaty (CTBT) there could be no normalisation in their bilateral relations.[10]

Even though, in terms of trade and investment, India-Japan relations began to make some headway during the 1980s and early 1990s, the political aspect of their relations yet had yet to recover from the shock of 1974. In 1998, India–more concerned about its immediate neighbourhood, particularly Pakistan and China–conducted five more nuclear tests at Pokharan bringing Indo-Japan relationship to its lowest ebb. The tests sent shockwaves across Japan which had so far provided considerable financial assistance to India. Japan, in response, intensified the financial 'measures' of condemning the tests by putting on hold various financial assistance programmes. Commenting on the effect of India's nuclear tests of 1998 on Indo-Japan relations, Japan's ambassador to India at the time Hiroshi Hirabayashi lamented: The test "was particularly perceived as a slap in the face by the Japanese people. To be frank, I was rudely shocked and felt betrayed by India, which I believed to be an anti-nuclear champion. Pokharan tests chilled our relationship to a great extent."[11] In response to Japan's severe condemnation of the tests, New Delhi asserted that the tests were conducted keeping in view India's core national security interests and that lecturing from Japan or Canada or Australia carry no weight since these countries themselves enjoy the safety of nuclear umbrella provided by their common patron, the United States.[12]

The bitterness caused by the nuclear tests of 1974 and 1998 notwithstanding, India-Japan relations witnessed a dramatic transformation with the onset of the twenty-first century. In this regard, Japanese Prime Minister Yoshiro Mori's visit to India in August 2000 proved to be a milestone in so far as it heralded the beginning of a qualitatively new chapter in Indo-Japan relations. The highlight of Prime Minister Mori's visit was his proposal to engage India in a 'Global Partnership' which would entail India and Japan joining hands to address issues pertaining not just to Asia, but to deepen their relations so that both countries could work together on 'wide ranging issues like UN reform, maritime security, combating terrorism and environment'.[13]

Since then, high-level official visits from both sides have increased in frequency and have immensely contributed to the cementing of bilateral relations between the two countries. For instance, the Joint Statement, signed by Indian Prime Minister Manmohan Singh and his Japanese counterpart Shinzo Abe in 2006, helped in upgrading the status of India-Japan relations from 'global partnership' to 'global and strategic partnership'–implying a joint effort by the two sides to widen the scope of India-Japan ties. The nomenclature change reflected growing cooperation between India and Japan as both nations were keen to take their bilateral relations beyond the 'economic and commercial' to include 'strategic and security' aspect as well. The Joint Statement also introduced, for the first time, the provision of annual prime ministerial summits which has so far provided the two countries with a mechanism to maintain and improve the momentum in their bilateral relations. Similarly, Japanese Prime Minister Shinzo Abe's visit to India from 25-27 January 2014 helped in furthering the cause of fostering close ties, and Abe was also accorded the honour of being the chief guest at the Republic Day parade in New Delhi.

The momentum in bilateral relations has been duly carried forward by Prime Minister Narendra Modi. Modi visited Japan from 30 August to September 3, 2014 where both sides further upgraded the status of Indo-Japan relations to 'Special Strategic and Global Partnership'. The visit was productive in so far as Japan showed willingness to increase the volume of investment in India with Prime Minister Abe promising to double the number of Japanese companies in India by the next five years. More recently, Japanese Prime Minister Shinzo Abe visited India in September 2107 and signed 15 agreements with his Indian counterpart in order to broaden the base of their strategic partnership. Both sides agreed to strengthen cooperation in the Indo-Pacific region where China is increasingly becoming assertive–a security concern shared both by India and Japan.[14] The talks between the two leaders were held in order to give boost to cooperation in various key sectors including civil aviation, trade, and science and technology. While addressing a joint press conference with Prime Minister Abe, Narendra Modi highlighted the salient feature of India-Japan strategic partnership by declaring that 'Indo-Japan ties are not limited to bilateral or regional spheres; the two sides also closely cooperate on key global issues'. Prime Minister Abe voiced the same spirit by asserting that India-Japan special strategic and global partnership was meant to drive peace and prosperity not just in Indo-Pacific region but for the whole world.[15]

The diplomatic energy spent by the two countries in forging closer cooperation has so far been productive as India-Japan relations continue to achieve new milestones with each passing year. However, both countries need to sustain and enrich their bilateral relations so as to be in a position to deal effectively with emerging challenges in the Indo-Pacific region and beyond.

Current Issues and Trends in India-Japan Relations

Even though India-Japan relations have remained constructive for the last seventeen years, the incumbent Prime Minister of India, Narendra Modi, and his Japanese counterpart, Shinzo Abe, need to be given credit for giving the bilateral relationship an unprecedented momentum. Abe's visit to India in September 2017, besides commencing the much-hyped Mumbai-Ahmedabad high-speed rail project, also reinvigorated the bilateral relations in other important areas. For instance, Japan was made a permanent member in the Malabar naval exercise which also involves the United States. Japan also signed a nuclear deal with India–Japan's first with a non-signatory of Nuclear Non-Proliferation Treaty (NPT). Further, a trilateral diplomatic arrangement at the foreign secretary level has also been put in place with Australia being the third country.[16] Moreover, India and Japan have also successfully started many high-profile projects like Delhi-Mumbai Industrial Corridor (DMIC) and Mumbai Trans-harbour link project which are under different stages of execution. Similarly, on the economic front, Japanese foreign direct investment and ODA to India have been witnessing a considerable rise in the recent years. Prime Minister Narendra Modi lauded the financial assistance provided by Japan in his speech at the India-Japan Business Leaders Forum in September 2017 by announcing that India received the highest ever ODA from Japan during 2016 and that "FDI flows from Japan have almost tripled in the last three years."[17]

Growing economic linkages aside, India and Japan share much when it comes to security and strategic environment in the Indo-Pacific region. In this regard, China's rise as a dominant actor becomes the most important issue confronting both India and Japan. Since there is an increasing power asymmetry between New Delhi and Beijing, it would be wise on the part of India not to try to act as a counterweight to China. Therefore, what India and Japan can do is to foster close relations among and between like-minded states who share apprehensions regarding China's increasing assertiveness in the region. In this regard, the 'Quad'–a group of four democracies, United States, India, Japan and Australia–can play a vital role in assuaging the concerns these countries share regarding China. At the same time, the Quad has the potential to build enough leverage so as to prevent Beijing from engaging in any sort of adventurism. Further, India and Japan would do well to foster closer cooperation with ASEAN countries since these nations are increasingly becoming over-dependent on Beijing. Towards this end, India, in particular, has made some significant headway in so far as India's Look East Policy has now been transformed as 'Act East Policy' under the hyperactive foreign policy outreach of Prime Minister Modi. India, by using its stature of being a democracy and a multicultural nation, and also by highlighting that New Delhi shares no dispute with any ASEAN country, can boost its association with ASEAN nations.[18] If New Delhi and Tokyo are in a position to entice ASEAN countries to shun their over-dependency on Beijing, then one can hope to see a rebalancing of power equation in Asia in favour of India and Japan.

Apart from the aforementioned mechanisms, India and Japan have displayed enough courage by launching the Asia-Africa Growth Corridor (AAGC) as a counterweight to the China-Pakistan Economic Corridor. The AAGC is aimed at 'promoting connectivity, infrastructure, and capacity-building across the Asia-Pacific community.'[19] The launching of AAGC reflects the unease that New Delhi and Tokyo share as far as Beijing's muscle flexing in the region is concerned. Similarly, India and Japan have also made significant progress in promoting bilateral maritime partnership in order to check China's 'expanding maritime presence from the Sea of Japan to the Indian Ocean rim.'[20]

However, India and Japan, while safeguarding their core national security interests, should avoid overt confrontation with China, for if so happens will only vitiate the already tenuous security environment in the region. Therefore, the focus of both New Delhi and Tokyo, as Professor Alam pertinently puts it, should be on 'widening the window of flexibility and opportunity in their conduct of foreign and security policies in Asia rather than seek an impossible containment of China that would provide no benefits to any party either in the short-term or long-term'. If cultivated carefully, India-Japan relations can truly becoming the defining relationship of the twenty-first century.

References

1. Swaran Singh, 'Why Is This Relationship So Special', *The New Indian Express*, 13 September 2017.
2. David M. Malone, *Does the Elephant Dance: Contemporary Indian Foreign Policy*, Oxford University Press, New Delhi, 2011, p. 201.
3. *Ibid.* pp. 202-203.
4. Arpita Mathur, *India-Japan Relations: Drivers, Trends and Prospects*, RSIS Monograph No. 23, 2012, p. 3.
5. *Ibid.*
6. R.B. Smith, "The Tokyo Conference and the Greater East Asia Perspective, 1943," in Chad J. Mitcham (ed.) *Changing Visions of East Asia 1943-93: Transformations and Continuities*, Routledge, London, 2007, p. 24.
7. The text of the treaty can be found at: http://www.commonlii.org/in/other/treaties/INTSer/1952/6.html (accessed on 29 November 2017).
8. Official Development Assistance was provided to India by Japan since 1958 as a result of the warmth created by the signing of Indo-Japan Peace Treaty. In fact, India was the first country to become the recipient of ODA From Japan.
9. David. M. Malone, op.cit. p. 211.
10. *Ibid.*
11. As cited in Arpita Mathur, *India-Japan Relations: Drivers, Trends and Prospects*, op.cit. p. 24.
12. *Ibid.*
13. *Ibid.* p. 25.
14. 'Shinzo Abe in India', *Indian Express,* September 14, 2017. Retrieved from: http://indianexpress.com/article/india/shinzo-abe-in-india-narendra-modi-heres-the-full-list-of-15-mous-and-agreements-signed-between-india-and-japan-4843456/ (Accessed on November 30, 2017).
15. *Ibid.*

16. 'India-Japan relations in good health', *Livemint*. Retrieved from http://www.livemint.com/Opinion/WGTtAfOQctuXMbOAUuolHP/IndiaJapan-relations-in-good-health.html (Accessed on November 30, 2017).
17. *Ibid.*
18. Swaran Singh, 'Rebooting India's Act East Policy', *The New Indian Express*, 15 November 2017.
19. Swaran Singh, 'Why Is This Relationship So Special', *The New Indian Express*, op.cit.
20. *Ibid.*
21. Mohammed Badrul Alam, "India-Japan Relations on a Roll: Evolving Strategies and Security Issues," in Mohammed Badrul Alam (ed.) *Contours of India's Foreign Policy: Changes and Challenges*, Reference Press, New Delhi, 2014, p. 180.

Chapter - 13

Indo-Japan Relations from the Lens of Soft Power

—Amit Kumar Gupta

India-Japan relations have received a tremendous fillip with numerous multilateral agreements being signed between the two governments in recent past. The duo now claim to be 'Special Strategic and Global Partners', cooperating in various fields, namely, disaster risk management, skills development, connectivity, economic and commercial, investment, civil aviation, science and technology, sports, academics, nuclear cooperation etcetera. Additionally, the two countries claim that Indo-Japan ties are not limited to bilateral or regional spheres only, but the two sides also closely cooperating on key global issues. This is evident from the Asia-Africa Growth Corridor (AAGC) initiative, which was launched by both India and Japan amid China's One Belt One Road (OBOR) project. The AAGC vision document seeks to connect Asia with Africa and consists of four main components: development and cooperation projects, quality infrastructure and institutional connectivity, capacity and skill enhancement and people-to-people partnerships. This AAGC initiative is part of Indo-Pacific freedom corridor that is being put in place by India and Japan with an eye on challenging and counterbalancing China's OBOR project (Chaudhury, 2017). To further strengthen cooperation in the Indo-Pacific region, the two countries together with the United States of America have been indulging themselves in the Malabar series of Naval drills that is meant to maintain the rule of law and maritime security in the region (Ramakrishnan, 2017).

However, with all said, it must be noted here that any understanding or reference to the Indo-Japanese relations is incomplete, if their soft power aspects are ignored. Both India and Japan are traditional allies and share a friendship that has a long history, which is deeply rooted in spiritual affinity and strong cultural and civilisational ties (MEA.Gov.in, 2015). Thus, one witnesses a heavy presence of soft power aspects in the relationship that the two countries share. Each of the two countries have their impressive potential soft power capabilities and resources, by means of which they are earning a name for themselves in the international platform. The practice and implementation of soft power resources to enhance their bilateral cooperation is very much visible in the foreign policies of India and Japan. Nonetheless, before analysing the use of soft power resources by the two countries, it first becomes essential to identify the soft power resources and potentials that the two countries possess.

India's Soft Power

India is one of the masters in the field of soft power. Its cultural enigma and exoticism, have attracted the imagination of numerous poets and thinkers, scientists and philosophers, intellectuals and masses all around the globe. India offers more than just something, and hence titillates everybody's pondering cognition. According to Mark Twain, India "is the land of dreams and romance, of fabulous wealth and fabulous poverty, of splendor and rags, of palaces and hovels, of famine and pestilence.... and the country of hundred nations and a hundred tongues, of a thousand religions and two million gods…the one land that all men desire to see, and having seen once, by even a glimpse, would not give that glimpse for the shows of all the rest of the world combined." Such paraphrases, in the praise of India's past are multitudinous. And, all this because of its rich medley–'multiplicity of languages and dialects gods and goddesses values and beliefs, customs and practices, sensuality and asceticism' (Singh, 1998; Gupta, 2013).

India possesses numerous unique qualities, or to put it in other words, it possess numerous soft power tools, which are enumerated as under:

1. Indian Culture

Culture is an effective soft power asset and is considered, as one of the essential instrument for projecting oneself to the world community, also while enhancing friendly ties with the foreign countries. Narratives of India's past show how cultural negotiations- the gifting of gems and jewellery, art objects and artifacts, the sharing of court poets, dancers, musicians, painters, sculptors, even cooks, craftspeople, weavers and etcetera, are records of how political issues have been resolved, or at least restrained, with help from things which are part of the cultural composite of a nation (Varma, 2008; Gupta, 2013).

India's cultural heritage is one of the most ancient and varied among all other cultural heritage of mankind. Throughout the ages, many races and peoples contributed to India's culture. Some came into contact only temporarily; while others settled permanently within its borders. The keynote of the distinctive culture thus evolved was synthesis on the basis of eternal values. (Chatterji *et.al.,* 1958) Indian culture has withstood the vagaries of time, and hence, has become even more enduring, insightful and ingenious which has so much to teach to the world. India is a 5000 year old civilisation now, and so are the components of its culture. People of different races came, intermingled with the already settled races, and presented a unique example of unity in diversity. (Singh 1998; Gupta 2013)

The multifarious components of Indian culture, which range from spiritualism, to art and craft, music, dance and drama, literature, cuisine, and many more, represents the aesthetic face of the world, that arouse a sensation which is not only incomprehensible but also intangible. They are as discussed below. (Gupta, 2013)

(a) Indian Spirituality

Topping the list of Indian soft power is its spirituality. Spiritual life is the true genius of India. It is believed that those who make the greatest appeal to the Indian mind are not the military conquerors, nor the rich merchants or the great diplomats, but the holy sages, the rishis who embody spirituality at its finest and purest form. India's pride is that almost in every generation and in every part of the country, from the time of her recorded history, she has produced these holy men who embody for her all that the country holds most dear and sacred. Though they generally remain away from the main stream of life, kings, noblemen and commoners pay reverence to them and take their advice in the problems of their personal lives as well as in public affairs. By their lives, they teach us that pride and power, wealth and glory, are nothing in comparison with the power of Spirit. (Chatterji *et.al.,* 1958)

India is believed to have influenced the Western imagination more because of its exotic and esoteric qualities, which is highlighted in its spirituality. Best examples here would be Steve Jobs experience of life-changing spiritual reflections in an India temple and similarly, Mark Zuckerberg's visit to India when Facebook was not doing very well. Simultaneously, you have scores of foreigners visiting India in search of solace and complete peace of mind. And the fact of the matter is that India does not have to fund its rishis and holy sages to highlight its soft power abroad.

India, as is also called the blessed land of gods, is that country, which has given birth to major religions of the world - Hinduism, Buddhism, Jainism and Sikhism. Christianity reached India, before it did to Rome or Europe. Islam too is in its full bloom. India's culture has absorbed all these religions with its followers living in harmony with one another - though with certain hiccups caused by political interests. Ignoring that, the rest have added to the richness of its culture and it represents a perfect archetype of 'unity in diversity'. These are the features that prompted the Tibetan Buddhist leader Dalai Lama to verbalise that "India's religious tolerance can be a role model for the rest of the world."

(b) The Indian Way of Life

Indian culture is richly reflected in the way its people live their lives. The evolution and growth of spirituality too is a result of the traditional Indian way of life. An Indian is expected to remember and bow to god first thing in the morning; indulge in yoga and meditation; never ever compromise on integrity for the purpose of prosperity; maintain strong bonds with the family members as well as relatives;

always take the advise of elders in case of any important decision; being hospitable to everyone who comes to your home; a young person is expected to touch the feet of his elders; he should always give respect to his elders and should not consume alcohol or smoke cigarettes….and the list continues.

Of all said, the predominant aspect of the Indian way of life, is the prevalent family values and the strong bond within the family members. It is this family bonding that prepares an Indian to lead a much contented and a happier life, than that compared to his rich counterparts in the West. The foreign nationals are very much enthralled by this Indian characteristic of strong bonding within the family. This prevalence of family values in India, presents India to the international community as a country, where love and brotherhood is thriving in abundance. This enhances India's image in the world community. Hence, it is blatantly visible that the Indian way of life, too can be portrayed as its much cherished soft power.

2. Indian medicine

Indian medicine share its genesis in the development of its culture, rooted deep into its ancient civilisational history, and is regarded as one of the oldest organised systems of medicine. Ayurveda, Naturopathy, Unani and Siddha forms of medicinal practices are Indian specialties. However, though India now is also walking the path of cutting-edge technology in healthcare, which is not just reliable but also cheap, as compared to its counterparts in the West, hereby attracting scores of foreign nationals to India for the purpose of treatment. (Gupta, 2013)

India is also one of the world's largest producers of generic drugs and vaccines, and additionally Indian companies like Ranbaxy and Dr Reddy's Laboratories are becoming well known around the world. The Government of India also claims that 'Polio' has been eradicated from India. All this goes to show how India's healthcare system and alternative medicinal systems raise India's intangible standing in the world community, and hence, proving to be India's efficient soft power tool.

3. Yoga

Talking of healthcare and alternative medicinal knowledge, Yoga, an Indian discovery, too is said to have answers, to all physical malaise. Citing a humble example, Indian yoga seems to be doing the dual work of bridging cultural ties between India and Nepal and also healing Prachanda, the Nepali Maoist leader, who is predominantly antagonistic to India. (*Ibid.*)

Now millions around the world practice yoga. There are attempts by various countries to patent various yoga positions as their own. This has always been opposed by India, as India is that country where yoga initially began. As a result of the present government of India's initiative the United Nations General Assembly has recognised 21st June as International Yoga Day, since 2015. Thus, it can be said without doubt that yoga can be one of the soft power tools of India, by means of which it can showcase India as a country that contributed to the world society a knowledge that would do a world of good to the people all over and all this at minimal or simply no monetary cost.

4. Indian Diaspora

Normatively, the values of love, peace and brotherhood are the qualities that Indians are known for, with Gautama Buddha, Mahavir, Ashoka and Mohandas Karamchand Gandhi being prime examples. At present, the Indian Diaspora seems to be winning the hearts of the world with their endearing demeanor and benign qualities. Sreeram Chaulia, in his article, 'The great Indian Diaspora', mentions that, "For the most part, an average American, Canadian or Dutchman does not see Indian immigrants as national security or economic threats, thanks to their humble, flexible and endearing qualities" (Chaulia, 2006). The Government of India has also recognised the contribution of its Diaspora to the development of India and has started celebration 'Pravasi Bharatiya Divas' on 9th January of every year, since 2003.

5. Indian Democracy

With 16 successfully conducted general elections, in a country of over 1.25 billion population, that too within a span of 70 years since independence, India does definitely boost itself as the largest democracy. This surprises many, especially to those who have seen most of the colonial Third World states failing in the political sphere and are living, or have lived in a state of political mayhem, with common citing of military dictatorships. India definitely is not without internal problems. Problems ranging from Naxalism to secessionist movements, insurgencies to state-sponsored terrorisms, communal riots to corruption; all these and more are a visible characteristic in India. However, India has withstood all, thanks to the resilient nature of Indian democracy. The people of India believe in democratic procedure, and do not at all hesitate to topple the party in power if it does not live up to the expectations of the people. Not begetting much surprise hence, the Indians boost of their democratic culture and the countries around the world are co opted into believing the uniqueness and grandeur of India and its democracy. (Gupta, 2013)

6. Indian Film Industry and Sports

Indian modern theatres and drama, is crossing all bounds and leaps that has found shape in the form of the Indian film industry, which now leads the world in film production with an average output of over 800 feature films a year. The Mumbai-based Hindi-language film industry, known as Bollywood, produces at least a quarter of these Indian movies. The Indian film Industry, is not just an entertainment industry, but is winning itself and for India, a name in the international platform, where the world is getting to know about India and its culture, through its films. Adding to the Indian drama and theatre industry, the recent entrant, the soap operas are also proving to be a large entertainment industry, not just in India, but also in South Asian, Southeast Asian countries, along with that of United Kingdom, United States of America, some countries of Europe, South Africa and Australia. These soap operas are already a big hit all across South Asia, Southeast Asia and among the Indian diaspora worldwide. Indian drama and theatre industry in all its forms seems to be gaining popularity and additionally winning the hearts all around, proving to be an effective soft power asset for India.

Likewise, in the field of sports, there are many like Vishwanathan Anand (Chess), Sachin Tendulkar (Cricket), Saina Nehwal and P.V. Sindhu (Badminton), Geet Sethi (Snooker), Abhinav Bindra (shooting), Mary Kom (boxing) and many more, who are doing India proud in the international platform.

Japan's Soft Power

> As the first non-Western country that drew even with the West in modernity while showing that it is possible to maintain a unique culture, Japan has more potential soft-power resources than any other Asian country. –Joseph S. Nye Jr., 2005.

The above remark by Joseph S. Nye Jr. gives us a glimpse of Japan's soft power potential, which can be further backed by the point that, "today Japan ranks first in the world in the number of patents, third in expenditure on research and development as a share of GDP, second in book sales and music sales, and highest for life expectancy." It is also home to three of the top 25 multinational brand names, namely, Toyota, Honda, and Sony. (Nye, 2005)

Most importantly the Government of Japan has begun to fund billions of yen to portray Japan's benign image in the international platform. In November 2013 the Japanese government launched the so-called 'Cool Japan Fund' to promote and portray Japanese culture abroad through the 'Cool Japan' campaign. The campaign supports the advertising and public relations, among other activities, so as to increase Japan's influence abroad. (Green, 2015)

Japanese comic books, animated videos, and pop music, are in high demand throughout the globe. This is understood to indicate that millions of people around the world are attracted to Japan's creative products, and the Japanese government wants to convert people's love of Japanese things into an attraction to Japan (*Ibid.*). The world consumers seem to be embracing all that, which is Japanese, such as, sushi, karaoke, rock garden, zen-inspired architecture, J-pop (popular music), J-fashion, electronic gizmos and games (Sony Play Station 3 and Nintendo), television dramas, manga (comics) and anime (cartoons). (Lam, 2007)

Japan is showcasing its image to the world through its soft power medium of manga and anime. The manga and anime set of series appear to have the best of both worlds, that is, distinctively Japanese in style and yet also have universal appeal among the young (Thorn, 2007). 'manga in Japanese signifies spontaneous picture. In fact, every sort of comic is referred to as manga. The world outside views 'manga' as those comic arts, which has its origin in Japan. 'Anime' are those animated films that are made in the same style as the manga books. Both are much more important for Japanese culture as the interest in manga is spread throughout all social stratums and all groups of professions. Even cookery books use manga to illustrate instructions. Generally, these manga and anime characters are characterised by their special physical features like big eyes, coloured hair and caricatured body. All these elements express meanings that is said to be recognised by the Japanese people only. (Layer, 2010)

Thus, it is visible that Japans cultural influence is very impressive, particularly among the younger generations. 'Playstation' have become more or less a household possession, and the Pokemon series is truly international in scope as it is broadcasted in more than 65 countries. According to Johan Ahlner, "these soft power resources allow Japan to play a kind of 'soft' hegemonic role, both through it popular culture but also through its massive outflow of ODA and FDI". (Ahlner, 2006)

Owing to Japan's economic robustness, its investment strength and strategy in the form of Official Development Assistance (ODA) and Foreign Direct Investment (FDI) can arguably be considered to be its most effective and significant soft power instrument. Japan has been the world's leading provider of ODA and FDI around the globe. The ODA program of Japan emphasizes on economic cooperation through trade credits, investment insurance and loan guarantees (Farell, 2008). Japan's ODA has helped improve the economic infrastructure of many developing countries around the world, which in turn attracted foreign investment in their respective countries, and increased production and export capacity brought about by the foreign investments. In such a manner, the Japanese investments have helped the economies of many countries. (Ministry of Foreign Affairs of Japan, n.d.)

In addition to its investment perks, it has also established the Japan Foundation in 1972 that seeks to promote Japanese language, arts and culture in foreign countries. The Foundation also promotes intellectual exchanges between Japan and the overseas countries. The Japan foundation is presently represented in Asia, Oceania, the Americas, Europe, Middle East and Africa. The Foundation has been very popular in promoting traditional Japanese artforms, like the austere 'Noh' theatre, 'Ikebana' (stylised flower arrangement), 'ukiyo-e' (woodblock prints) and the 'Zen' inspired tea ceremony, which are popularly very exquisite, refined and quaint. The Japan Foundation works in tandem with the Ministry of Foreign Affairs to promote pop culture like manga and anime for greater international outreach. (Lam, 2007)

Evidences of Soft Power in Indo-Japan Relations

As has been evident, both India and Japan have their strengths in their unique soft power, which they seem to have been implementing so as to improve their bilateral ties. The close cooperation between India and Japan has a long history, which is deeply rooted in spiritual affinity and strong cultural ties. Historians claim that India's earliest contact with Japan was with the Todaiji Temple in Nara, where the consecration or eye-opening of the statue of Lord Buddha was performed by an Indian monk, Bodhisena, in 752 AD (Embassy of India, Tokyo Website, 2017). However, some other scholars like Richard John Bowring, claim that Buddhism has been practiced in Japan, since it was introduced in the year 552 BC (Bowring, 2005). Thus, it is evident that cultural exchanges between the two countries began with the introduction of Buddhism to Japan from India. In the contemporary period, we had other prominent Indians who were very closely associated with Japan, namely, Swami Vivekananda, Gurudev Rabindranath Tagore, JRD Tata, Netaji Subhash Chandra Bose, Radha Binod Pal and etcetera. Henceforth, the Japan-India Association was set up in 1903, which is today the oldest international friendship association in Japan. Over the years, both India and Japan have built upon their traditional values and created a partnership based on both their idealism and pragmatism. Today, India claims to be the largest democracy and Japan the most prosperous in Asia. (Embassy of India, Tokyo Website, 2017).

Amidst, strong cooperation in the fields of polity, economy and science and technology, both India and Japan have been working towards further strengthening their ties in the cultural sphere. Post-Indian independence, a cultural agreement was first signed between India and Japan in October 1956. Prior to the agreement, in 1951, India had initiated a scholarship system for young Japanese scholars who could study in India. In April 1988, Indian Prime Minister Rajiv Gandhi attended the opening ceremony of the Festival of India in Japan. This was followed by the inauguration of the Vivekananda Cultural Centre in Tokyo, which was opened in September 2009. The Centre offers classes on varied fields, such as, Yoga, musical classes which include, 'Tabla' and both classical and Bollywood dances. The Centre also offers Hindi and Bengali languages. Similarly, the Indian Council for Cultural Relations has set up two Chairs on India studies at Ryukoku University, Reitaku University, in Japan. To further strengthen cultural ties, a year-long Festival of India in Japan 2014-15 was held from October 2014 to September 2015. Likewise, on 18th June, 2017, various events were organised in Japan on the occasion of the 3rd International Day of Yoga. The year 2017, has been designated as the 'Year of Friendly Exchanges' by the two countries. Other most important component in the Indo-Japan relationship are the Indian Diaspora in Japan, who by dint of their hard work and skills are earning a name for themselves and for India in Japan (Embassy of India, Tokyo Website, 2017). Additionally, India is among the largest recipient of Japan's essential soft power tool, that is, its Official Development Assistance (ODA). One must thus conclude that soft power plays a dominant role in the Indo-Japan robust relationship.

References

1. Ahlner, Johan. (2006). Japan's Soft Power: An Unsustainable Policy? Lund University Libraries, [Online Web] Accessed: November 07, 2017, URL: https://lup.lub.lu.se/student-papers/search/publication/1326099
2. Bowring, Richard John. (2005). *The Religious Traditions of Japan, 500-1600*. UK, Cambridge University Press.
3. Chatterji, Sunita Kumar, Dutt, Nalinaksha, Pusalker A.D. and Bose, Nirmal Kumar (eds.). (1958). *The Cultural Heritage of India: The Early Phases (Prehistoric Vedic and Upanishadic, Jaina and Buddhist),* Volume I, Calcutta, published by Swami Lokeswarananda, Secretary, The Ramakrishna Mission, Institute of Culture.

4. Chaudhury, Dipanjan Roy. (May 26, 2017). India, Japan Come up with AAGC to Counter China's OBOR. *The Economic Times*.
5. Chaulia, Sreeram. (2006). The Great Indian Diaspora. *Overseas Indian: connecting India with its Diaspora*, official e-Zine of ministry of Overseas Indian Affairs, , (Online Web) Accessed November 18, 2017, URL: http://www.overseasindian.in/2006/feb/news/opinion24.shtml.
6. Farrel, Roger. (2008). *Japanese Investment in the World Economy: A Study of Strategic Themes in the Internationalisation of Japanese Industry*. Edward Elgar Publishing.
7. Green, H. Steven. (2015). The Soft Power of Cool: Economy, Culture and Foreign Policy in Japan. [Online Web] Accessed: November 06, 2017, URL: https://www.google.co.in/url?sa=t&rct=j&q=&esrc=s&source=web&cd=1&cad=rja&uact=8&ved=0ahUKEwiozM-hse3XAhXCJcAKHYHPBRkQFggmMAA&url=https%3A%2 F%2Ftoyo.repo.nii.ac.jp%2F%3Faction%3Drepository_action_common_download%26item_id%3D7228%26item_no%3D1%26attribute_id%3D22%26file_no%3D1&usg=AOvVaw10teR67LslckqT02MrBs8k
8. Gupta, Amit Kumar. (June-December, 2013). Soft Power of the United States, China and India: A Comparative Analysis. *Indian Journal of Asian Affairs*, Vol. 26, No. 1/2, Jaipur, pp. 37-57.
9. Lam, Peng Er. (2007). Japan's Quest for 'Soft Power': Attraction and Limitation. *East Asia*, 24, Springer, pp. 349-363.
10. Layer, Stefanie. (2010). An Exploration of Japan's Soft Power: A Case Study About Japan's use of manga and anime. [Online Web] Accessed: November 06, 2017, URL: http://www.culturaldiplomacy.org/pdf/case-studies/manga-and-anime-an-exploration-of-japans-soft-power.pdf
11. MEA.Gov.in. (July, 2015). India – Japan Relations, [Online Web] Accessed: November 12, 2017, URL: https://www.mea.gov.in/Portal/ForeignRelation/Japan_2015_07_23.pdf
12. Ministry of Foreign Affairs of Japan. (n.d.). Official Development Assistance, [Online Web] Accessed: November 17, 2017, URL: http://www.mofa.go.jp/policy/oda/summary/1995/2approaches.html.
13. Nye, Joseph S. (December 5, 2005). Soft Power Matters in Asia. The Japan Times. [Online Web] Accessed: November 17, 2017, URL: https://www.belfercenter.org/publication/soft-power-matters-asia.
14. Ramakrishnan, T. (July 14, 2017). Malabar Drills Aim at Giving Regional Security, says Japan. *The Hindu*.
15. Singh, B. P. (1998). *India's Culture: The State, the Arts and Beyond*, Delhi, Oxford University Press.
16. Thorn, Matt. (March, 2007). Manga Mania. Japan Plus: *Asia-Pacific Perspectives*, Vol.4. No. 11, pp. 3-21.

17. Varma, Pavan K. (2008). Culture as an Instrument of Diplomacy. *Indian Foreign Affairs Journal, A Quarterly of the Association of Indian Diplomats,* Volume 3, No. 2, New Delhi, Cambridge University Press India Pvt. Ltd.

Index

N

T